The Devil in the Detail

Seven lively tales for seven deadly sins

Paul Beck

ISBN: -10: 1502902710

ISBN-13: 978-1502902719

To Jenifer, who has helped me in this, and all my endeavours, more than I can say

Table of Contents

My inspiration for these seven tales comes from the ancient notion of the seven deadly sins.

The tales are fables that help us see what we fail to see, heed to what we fail to hear, as we go about our daily lives.

It is a truism that we are all sinners. When we sin we hurt those close to us. But because they are close we try to soften the blow, provided we have kind hearts.

But there are those who are given power or who take it for themselves. And however trivial that power, they can inflict suffering. It often seems that those with power do not care what pain they inflict.

As far as I know, it is only the medical profession that acknowledges that its members can damage lives as they go about their business. Doctors are required to reflect before they decide what to do. They apply three tests:

*   first do no harm

*   it may be better to do nothing than to cause more harm than good

*   ensure that the cure is not worse than the ill.

In contrast, officials and lawmakers are slow to appreciate how harmful their actions can be. They do little to lessen the suffering they cause. To add insult to injury, they are masters at hiding their mistakes and sliding away from responsibilities.

So what's new? Well, there is something new. Ever since the 'defeat' of the totalitarian regimes of the Soviet world, the imperative to foster openness and equality appears to be withering away. Freedoms, hard-won over two centuries, have been eroded in the democracies of the West. An important function of these freedoms is to ensure that authorities are scrutinised and controlled. Without freedom it is hard or impossible to rescue individuals from those who misuse their power.

Various explanations are offered as our freedoms are curtailed, mostly the 'unprecedented' threat from terrorism. But this threat is far from unprecedented. The IRA was an ever-present danger for decades in the British Isles; now its former leaders participate in government. The Algerian war wrought havoc in France. The Basque country has been ravaged by terrorist violence for many years. Most countries in Africa suffered 'terrorist' insurgency until the colonial powers granted independence; in many African countries, former terrorists were reclassified as freedom fighters.

What is different today is that terrorists have struck at the United States, which had previously thought itself immune. US citizens, who had never seen themselves as oppressors, felt aggrieved to be a target for revenge. It is natural for people who believe they are innocent victims to want to fight back. But experience has shown that battling against terrorists is usually futile, that smarter strategies are needed to neutralise the threat.

A war on terrorism has been declared: a dirty and difficult war, a war which requires exceptional sacrifice. Governments are using the smoke-screen of security to dismantle some of the safeguards which have been painfully constructed since the birth of modern democracy in the 18th century, safeguards put in place because of the temptation faced by holders of power to tighten their grip and oppress the population.

. . .

These stories have a modest objective. They are intended to remind us of the home-grown dangers that 'the authorities' can bring. Just as the driver of a car is said to be in charge of a lethal weapon, the holder of office has the means to injure and maim. Power brings temptation, even to the best intentioned. Routine renders the holders of office insensitive to the pain they inflict, often encouraged by their supervisors in the name of efficiency. The drudgery of dealing with tens or hundreds of cases every week leads officials to objectify their clients to preserve distance. Sympathy and empathy, the cornerstones of decency, are washed away.

Some officials are attracted to their jobs because they

crave power: the pleasure of making others bend to their will, enhanced status, and the opportunity to gain financial and other advantage. Even those who do not set out to benefit from perks may develop a taste for them. Or they may be seduced by a culture which takes benefits for granted and requires that all members take part so that any potential whistle blower is isolated.

My personal *bête noire* is those people who "know best" and seek positions which give them the power to impose their will. When officials act thoughtlessly, they can hurt those of us who simply want to enjoy our lives, make few waves, and (to mix two metaphors) leave behind the faintest of footprints.

The third tale, about greed, is different from the others. Avarice, power and wealth form a self-reinforcing complex that rarely gets the attention it deserves. The seriously greedy are obliged to participate in the power structure; this is essential if they are to continue to accumulate and preserve their wealth. The rise of the family dynasty in *The Man Who Stole Bryce Canyon* shows how power is brokered – and how it provides the backdrop against which events in the other tales are played out.

. . .

On holiday recently, I watched a news item on CNN. The head teacher of an English primary school had begun to take her small white dog into school. The children were delighted and the little terrier was allowed to wander the classrooms and corridors. The pupils and staff became very fond of it. All was well until an official inspection was carried out and the inspector ruled, without explanation, that dogs were not allowed on school premises. This was a blow to the whole school community.

As it happened, my holiday reading was *Austerlitz* by W.G. Sebald (translated from the German by Anthea Bell). And shortly before watching the CNN news item, I had read the following passage.

Of course, it was much harder for Agata ... to manage under the new regime. Since the Germans had issued their decrees on the Jewish population (of Prague), she could go shopping only at certain times; she must not take

9

a taxi, she could sit only in the last carriage of the tram, she could not visit a coffee-house or cinema, or attend a concert or any other event...

in the late autumn of 1941, ... Agata had to take her wireless, her gramophone and the records she loved so much, ... to the so-called Compulsory Collection Centre. Because of some mistake she had made in complying with this order, she was sent to shovel snow...

...the two envoys of the Israelite religious community whom she had been expecting for some time arrived with the news that Agata must prepare to be taken away ... and gave her a sheaf of printed forms and instructions setting out everything down to the very smallest detail: where and when the person summoned must present herself, what items of clothing were to be brought - coat, raincoat, warm headgear, ear muffs, mittens, nightdress, underclothes, and so on ... the weight of the main item of luggage, which was not to exceed fifty kilos; ... the proviso that all the attached forms were to be filled in and signed, ... and all orders issued by the official authorities were to be followed to the letter in every contingency.

This description, horrific in its detail, was the outcome of a series of decisions. These decisions were made by politicians and implemented by an army of officials charged with building the structure and working out the practical details of deciding who was to be affected, and how and when those affected should comply with the legal requirements imposed on them. And – chillingly – there were those who sat in their offices and designed the forms.

The behaviour of the Nazis before and during the Second World War is a cliché of evil. The war was fought to ensure that it should never happen again. But I want you to consider that the bureaucratic structures, and the individuals who manned them, were ordinary men and women, little different from those who enforced racial segregation in the United States up to and through the 1960s, or who administered colonial power in Africa up to the 1960s, or who removed half-caste children from their Aboriginal mothers in Australia up to the 1970s, or who held young women in Magdalene

Laundries in Ireland up to 1996. And they are still used today to enforce the relatively small-scale but ferocious control of refugees who seek asylum in Britain.

There was a difference between what was done in Prague, as described in *Austerlitz*, and the school inspector's ruling about the little white dog. The school inspector was not enforcing the law; he was acting on a whim. The head teacher who sought to add colour to the life of her school also had the will to fight back. She appealed against the decision and continued to bring the dog into school. A second inspector overturned the ruling of the first because it had no basis in law. But what happened to the Jews in Prague was backed by law from which there was no appeal.

The question that I ask myself is this. What was first inspector thinking when he chose to restrict the freedom of the school, its head, its staff and its children?

This is what I have tried to bring to life in these seven tales. I want to dramatise events so we can see a little more clearly. If we can grasp what is happening, perhaps we can each make our tiny contribution to making the world a more humane place.

Power should be exercised with humility and compassion. And we should all be eternally vigilant in our scrutiny of those who exercise power over us: from the law-makers down to the officials and administrators.

We live in a complex world and are tempted to objectify the problems that beset us. We blame "them" for the raft of ills that we face every day. I want us to be reminded that "they" are individual people who choose to do what they do. And what they do can damage lives.

The offer of security is an illusion. No system, however draconian, can protect from random acts of violence. But the damage caused by loss of freedom is a certainty. Just ask a black South African who lived under apartheid or a Palestinian trying to live under a regime of oppression in Gaza.

The characters in these stories are fictional. But – sadly – many of the narratives are based on fact.

In which the GLUTTON overindulges
without devouring the tiniest morsel

Belinda glanced at the clock above the tobacco display as she waited to pay for her groceries. She scanned the scene around her. Directly before her in the queue, the bottom half of a tracksuit struggled to contain the hips of a woman with a small boy at her side. Belinda sighed with irritation as he pulled the strap that closed off the check-out and snapped it back: in and out, in and out, in and out.

The shop had opened six months earlier and each time Belinda visited, it seemed, the same woman was there. And each time she looked larger. She wore an anorak with fake-fur edging that tufted into untidy spikes. It gaped to reveal a pink T-shirt with a bunny motif. Belinda noticed such details; she could not stop herself counting things. It's what made her so good at her job. She gazed at the selection of cheap food filling the woman's trolley: two large bottles of cola, a box of microwave burgers and another of angel cake, two trays of sausage rolls, a can of rice pudding, two cans of hot dogs, three packets of chocolate biscuits, a bag of oven chips, and a jumble of confectionery bars.

When she arrived at the till, the woman asked for twenty cigarettes. It took time to sort out her shopping and collect her son, so she and Belinda left the shop at the same time.

Belinda turned left towards the complex of new houses and flats overlooking the water, home to city types like herself, relative newcomers to the area. The fat lady turned right, setting off towards what remained of the council estates and workmen's cottages left stranded amongst the smart Docklands' developments of the 1980s and 90s.

The post had arrived in Belinda's flat, a large envelope from Savills estate agents. Her hands were full, so she gripped it in her teeth and carried it into the living room, before dropping it on the sofa. She hurried into her gleaming but rarely-used kitchen to unload her shopping. It didn't take long: a bottle of mineral water, two packets of prepared salad leaves and a plastic box containing cooked and peeled prawns.

She returned to the living room. Light poured in from the plate-glass windows overlooking a small marina with the river beyond. The brochure from Savills was printed on thick, glossy paper that smelt like a fashion magazine. Her eyes searched the pages. The 'spectacular, top-floor, loft-style' apartment had a 9 ft. by 8 ft. walk-in wardrobe. She smiled, dialled the number on her iPhone and arranged a viewing.

It was time to go. She locked up, skipped down five flights of stairs and made her way to the Dockland's Light Railway.

· · ·

Tracy and Darren, her son, arrived home to a flat on the third floor of a council block. Tracy dropped her shopping, extracted the angel cakes and sausage rolls, collapsed on the sofa, and turned on the television. She had an appointment too; she was expecting a visit from someone official.

The letter had arrived a couple of weeks earlier. Tracy was coming to the end of her entitlement to job seeker's allowance and now some nosey parker was coming to check up on her. Her stomach churned as the doorbell rang. She heaved herself off the sofa, sent her Darren to answer the door, and went to make tea.

· · ·

Rosemary always made an effort with her appearance. Her job was to ginger up those who had relied on the State for too long. She dressed to give herself an edge. To intimidate, just a little. A three-day course had taught her how to deal empathetically with 'clients'. She knew how to let them talk, 'to give them plenty of rope to hang themselves,' as the affable young instructor had explained. She knew how to avoid dropping bombshells during meetings, and to convey bad news – cuts in benefits and so on – by letter. The course had devoted a whole afternoon to avoiding confrontation and to personal safety.

Darren led her into the sitting room. Rosemary was irritated by the television but it kept the boy occupied so she said nothing. She accepted a cup of tea from Tracy, whose hand was trembling as she proffered a slice of cake, still in its box.

Rosemary began in a carefully-practised tone. 'So, Tracy. Can I call you Tracy? Tell me about yourself.'

'I've always been big,' Tracy began, 'but never like this. I got three GCSE's at school and then got a job at Miller's sewing leather parts for car seat covers. It was regular work and they was kind to us even though the money wasn't too good. I married when I was eighteen and Darren came along a few months after. Joe, is dad, got a job on the oil rigs. The money would set us up, he said. The second time he was up there, he killed himself on his motorbike on his way home. So that put the kibosh on that.'

'That's awful,' said Rosemary. She raised her head to look at Tracy. She was accustomed to abandoned mothers but widowhood at such a young age was new to her. 'How on earth did you cope?' she asked.

'Well, I was lucky in a way 'cos we'd got the flat and Miller's had this scheme which let us choose our own hours. I could look after Darren and go on working with a bit of help from me mum. A job like that don't come easy. Most girls, once they was up the duff, went straight on the welfare.'

'It must have been hard for you, going out to work with the boy to look after.'

'Dad always said, 'You're better off working, gal. You don't have to kow-tow to no bloody toffee-nosed busybodies from the social.' No offence meant. And that's what I wanted. But about a year ago now, we got called to the canteen. I didn't know what they was on about, something about the company being taken over by some big American outfit. Miller's was being shut down. We'd all get our cards. You don't get much warning, do you? I was lucky. I got two months' wages and a bit of holiday money and that was that.'

Tracy paused, helped herself to another cake and stared

15

into the distance. Her eyes moistened. 'I heard on the news that night, the name of the American outfit, Constipated Equipment or somefink. And how only a hundred and fifty jobs was lost.'

Rosemary thought it best not to laugh. She tried to look sympathetic.

'Easy to say: only a hundred and fifty, if the job ain't yours,' Tracy continued, her voice cracking.

'It's alright, Tracy, I do understand.'

'So I went down the labour, job centre, some effin' name or other. It'd be better if they had bloody jobs instead of changing the effin' name. Anyway, I went down and signed on. Job Centre effin'Plus, that's it. Stupid fuckin' name. Excuse me language. I went for loads of jobs but it's Darren, you see. Mum's not well and I can't ask her to do much. I've been to ten interviews but none of them could match the hours for Darren. I've always worked. I get miserable sittin' here just watching the telly.'

Tracy's eyes overflowed; tears spilled down her cheeks. She reached for the last cake in the box but changed her mind. Instead she pulled open a drawer in the coffee table and rifled about until she found a Snickers bar. She tore off the wrapper and took a large bite. Rosemary watched as she wiped chocolate from the corner of her mouth and bit off another large chunk. Her jowls quivered as she chewed. It was hardly surprising she was so enormous.

'I started stuffin' me face to cheer myself up, let myself go. I couldn't be bothered to cook for me or Darren. Crisps and pork pies we had most nights, sometimes fish and chips. Mum took me down the quack. She gave me pills for depression. I'm on 'em now. It got me off me fat arse and down the shops to buy stuff to cook. Only microwave, mind. Then I started going for jobs again. When I was down, I couldn't be fussed. But when I went for jobs, I could see people lookin'. I was only sixteen stone then but you could see 'em thinkin', we're not giving a job to that fat bitch.'

Tracy finished the Snickers, screwed up the wrapper and dropped it into a bin half full of discarded food packaging and used tissues. She pulled an ash tray towards her and opened her packet of Pall Mall.

'D'you wanna fag?'

Rosemary shook her head.

Tracy lit up and sucked the smoke deep into her chest. Rosemary felt torn as she watched her struggle with a brief coughing fit. Tracy had indeed been dogged by bad luck. Her desire to stand on her own feet seemed genuine. But her self-indulgence was ugly.

'All I could do was sit here with the bloody telly doin' bugger all. Darren's a good boy and he loves his mum but it's not much of a life. What can I do? Thinkin' about what'll 'appen to him makes it worse. And then I look out the window and see girls what have never done an honest day's work and been on the social from the start. Larfin' and enjoying theyselves. They couldn't give a fuck. Excuse me language. Then I think, what's wrong with me? Did Dad get it wrong? 'Cos when you go down the road and see all them poncy types with flash 'ouses and flash cars, you realise you ain't got a chance – you might as well give up. Take what's going.'

Tracy was agitated, her face flushed. Darren remained glued to the television watching one cartoon after another, each with its own jolly jingle.

Rosemary struggled with an unwelcome feeling of sympathy. She was usually more than happy to disappoint her clients but she was finding it difficult to believe that Tracy was a sponger. She tidied her papers to avoid looking at her; what had to be said could be left to the standard follow-up letter. A true professional, she squashed her feelings and left Tracy with a few leaflets and a form to complete. She began to compose a report in her head as she descended the stairs.

. . .

Belinda's friend, Rachel was waiting for her at a shiny black table in a waterfront salad bar. Belinda travelled the two short stops to their rendezvous on the Docklands Light Railway.

'How was your trip?' asked Rachel as she greeted Belinda with a hug. 'You've been away a week, haven't you?'

'Yes, it was *fabulous*. I *had* to tell you about it.'

They were the only two women in their department at the bank and they clung to each other for mutual support in the chauvinist atmosphere.

The waiter helped Belinda slip off her dark grey tailored coat, revealing a scarlet dress with broad shoulders and a square neck. The cut of the dress made the most of her barely perceptible curves. Heads turned in the salad bar.

Belinda smiled. 'I got it in Manhattan. Gorgeous, isn't it?'

'Wonderful,' said Rachel, staring at the dress.

Only if you're borderline anorexic, she thought.

As soon as she sat down, Belinda launched into an account of the fat woman in the supermarket.

'I don't know how people get like that,' she said in a penetrating voice. 'They can't have any self control. They end up with diabetes and guess who has to pay for their medication? They don't know how to look after their kids, so along comes another generation of layabouts. I bet she doesn't even work. It's you and me that have to feed that fat face of hers, you can bet on it.'

She ordered a watercress and rocket salad with no dressing, a slice of smoked salmon and a bottle of Swedish mineral water. Rachel asked for a light dressing on her asparagus, and blinis with her caviar. Her eyes had been drawn to more substantial items on the menu but she failed to curb her impulse to compete with Belinda's abstinence.

'You know we get the lowest bonuses in the office,' Belinda continued, 'and we work every bit as hard as the men. Harder, probably. Peter and his cronies go out to lunch every day. I know they're not out for long but I eat salad at my desk. It has been months since my bonus was paid and I've been itching to go to New York for a bit of retail therapy. I've only just managed to fit it in.'

Rachel gave an understanding nod. She was about to interject but wasn't quick enough to seize the initiative. Belinda surged on.

'Every time something crops up, Peter asks me to start

18

the research. I know for a fact that I put out twice as many research notes as any man in that office. And they have the cheek to give us smaller bonuses.'

At this point, she lowered her voice to a whisper. 'John has only been with us for nine months and he got *half a million*. And do you know what they gave me? A miserly three hundred thousand. By the time I've paid tax, it's only a hundred and eighty.'

Her voice rose again. 'And they've the cheek to say it's because I don't get involved in face-to-face negotiations. Chance would be a fine thing. Peter's a total creep. He'd never let me out of the office at all if he thought he could get away with it. *You girls*, he says, *you haven't got the balls*. And then makes creepy comments about make-up and nail polish, trips to the loo and PMT. God, I hate him. And all the time he never takes his eyes off my chest.'

Rachel watched in silence as Belinda picked at her salad and sipped her water.

'I had a fabulous time in New York. I wish you could have come with me. I stayed at the Palace on Madison Avenue, a Tower Corner Suite. I always stay there, it's so luxurious. I order an aroma therapy massage the moment I arrive. They come to your room so you're left with wonderful smells. And I have another every day after shopping.'

Rachel never indulged herself so extravagantly. She wished there was someone less gross with whom she could form an alliance in the office. And now there was a new source of resentment. She shifted uncomfortably on her chair.

'I love shopping in New York.' Belinda continued. 'I started at Tiffany's.'

She picked up her handbag.

'Look at this! I got it while I was there. Isn't it lovely? It's a Nancy Gonzales. Real crocodile. Almost four thousand dollars but worth it, don't you think?'

She caressed the expensive leather, then opened the bag and searched inside. Her hand emerged clutching a velvet jewel box. Nestled inside was a dark blue enamel bracelet.

'I saw this on the internet. It's a Schlumberger. But there's nothing like actually buying it at Tiffany's.'

She took the bracelet out of its case and clipped it on her wrist, offering it up for Rachel to admire. Rachel ran her fingers across the swirls of gold inlaid into the enamel. She thought of the collection of antique jewellery left to her by her grandmother.

Belinda withdrew her arm, stared fondly at the bracelet contrasting with her milk-white skin, and returned it to its box. Rachel remained silent.

'Then I went on a trip round all the best boutiques. That's when I got the handbag.'

Belinda opened the clasp and dropped the velvet box inside.

'They call them purses over there. There's no end of fashionable places. With new ones opening all the time, it's hard to keep up, even though I get all the magazines. I'll give you a tip. If you stay at a really top-notch hotel, the concierge keeps a list of what's hot. Where the really smart people go. And then you get a hotel limo to ferry you around. This time, I bought seven dresses, five pairs of shoes, two handbags, two coats, and four embroidered jackets.'

And a partridge in a pear tree, thought Rachel.

'How lovely,' she said, staring at her empty plate.

A shadow had passed across her face when Belinda mentioned her bonus. Now she raised the subject again.

'How did you get three hundred thousand?' she asked. 'I only got two.'

Belinda flushed. 'It was that Consolidated Equipment deal. Don't you remember? It took eight months to coax them into buying In-Car-Supplies. In the end, we got them to pay a premium of forty-five percent over the stock market price. We had to work really hard to convince them it was worth the money. I wrote a report which showed that In-Car did most of its manufacturing in Britain and there would be huge savings if they moved production offshore.'

She lowered her voice. 'The really smart move was putting

out a press release saying that only a hundred and fifty jobs would be lost in the UK. It was nine hundred in the end. All hell would have broken loose if that had come out before the deal went through. But no-one follows up once it's done and dusted.'

Rachel shifted again on her chair.

'Don't take it too hard,' said Belinda. 'I really worked for it *and* I had to twist Peter's arm to get the three hundred. He also agreed to let me put the New York fare and hotel on expenses – as long as I called into the office over there for ten minutes or so. That's how it came to be a business trip.'

And that's supposed to make me feel better? thought Rachel

'Why don't you come round next week and I'll show you the things I've bought. And come with me to look at a new flat I've got my eye on. The one I've got is OK but the wardrobes are stuffed to the gunnels. I need more space. It's a pity they've stopped Concorde. First class is OK but, if Concorde was flying, I'd go across the pond more often. Why don't you come with me? Come soon. We'll have a brilliant time.'

Rachel mumbled and bit her lip. They drank skinny lattes and prepared to leave the table.

'Wasn't there a subsidiary of In-Car-Supplies round here somewhere?' asked Rachel as they put on their coats.

'Yes,' said Belinda 'I went to have a look. Have you actually seen any of the businesses you've dealt with? It's a real eye opener. I wouldn't do it too often but this one was just a couple of stops on the DLR, not one of those godforsaken places in the Midlands or the North. It was a terrible dump. I don't know how anyone could bear to work there. It had the most appalling productivity. I think it was the first factory to go when the takeover went through and production moved to China. Human resources was a complete shambles. The staff got away with murder. Do you know, they actually had flexitime on the shop floor? Mitchell's, I think it was called. No, Miller's. It was called Miller's. They made car seat covers.'

Bully Boys

In which unrighted wrongs lead

to an explosion of ANGER

When Joan Hunter was wheeled into Accident and Emergency, her left eye was closed and swollen, blood was congealed beneath her nostrils, and the left side of her jaw was bruised. She clutched her chest and winced each time she moved.

Patients with such injuries were common on Saturday nights, but today was Wednesday, it was eleven o'clock in the morning and Miss Hunter, unlike most victims of a beating, was middle-aged and wore a smart suit. Smart, that is, until the jacket was stained with blood.

The ambulance driver helped the head teacher of Nelson Mandela High move from one trolley to another, while the paramedic who had prattled pleasant nonsense to keep up her spirits went to fetch her a glass of water. A triage nurse arrived and closed the curtains for privacy. She asked for Miss Hunter's name, put a tag on her wrist, and asked how she was feeling. She examined her bruised eye and nose, felt her ribs, and completed an X-ray form.

'I don't think there's anything seriously wrong,' she said, 'but an X-ray will show if you've cracked any ribs. Looking in the mirror won't be fun for a while.'

As the nurse went out, she ushered in two police constables who were waiting to take a statement. They had been summoned by the school secretary who told them of the commotion in the head teacher's study when Mr Wilson was in a meeting with Miss Hunter. She had heard raised voices and then a scream. She had rushed into the study just as the second door to the corridor slammed shut. The desk was in disarray and Miss Hunter was slumped in her chair clutching her face.

23

A straightforward case, thought the officers, an easy job. But Miss Hunter refused to give a statement

. . .

Problems had begun the previous January, shortly before Miss Hunter reluctantly accepted the job of acting head of Nelson Mandela School in South London. The school's catchment area was a large estate managed by a housing association. Its academic standards were below average but not too bad. The previous head, Mr Scarfell, had maintained good discipline by ruthless use of exclusion, the only weapon that remained in his armoury.

Mr Scarfell's approach was old fashioned; corporal punishment was still in use during his early years as a teacher. As time passed, he had weaned himself off the cane but he retained a natural authority and had no difficulty imposing his will. He liked the children, including the difficult ones, and his dominance was tempered with fairness. He put himself out to push the able children forward, while those who misbehaved were always given a second chance. But he was ruthless with those who refused to toe the line after he had made the effort to explain how they should behave. He believed that it was his duty was to protect children who wanted to work from those who were bent on disruption.

Miss Hunter did not approve of Mr Scarfell's approach. She would have preferred a more liberal regime

. . .

When Robert Harding was appointed head of Children's Services in the local authority, he was attracted by the ethos of a council that changed the name of the school from Grubb Street Comprehensive to Nelson Mandela High.

He soon spotted Mr Scarfell's high level of exclusions. He called him to a meeting and gave him a clear instruction: he would not stand by and watch as children were denied a place in his schools. He was also disappointed with the school's academic performance. Mr Scarfell explained that the school's intake was poor and produced statistics which showed that pupils made excellent progress in his care.

But Mr Harding had a hidden agenda. When he was

preparing his job application, he had come across an incident which happened a few years earlier. A male member of staff at Nelson Mandela had been accused of sexual assault by a schoolgirl with a history of truancy, trouble-making and insubordination. The girl was not very bright and her accusation was riddled with inconsistencies. Nothing could be proved. The police dropped the case but the local authority, which had a zero-tolerance policy towards sexual harassment and rather vague procedures for investigation, tried to sack the teacher. He was defended by Mr Scarfell who, after a bruising battle, succeeded in excluding the girl and reinstating his member of staff.

Mr Harding, in his new role as head of Children's Services, wanted no trouble-makers. Even before his feet were under the desk, he had decided to get rid of Scarfell. In the event, he was pushing at an open door.

Close to retirement age, Mr Scarfell had had enough of writing and rewriting the school's plans and strategies with every new government initiative. These directives seemed to emerge on an almost monthly basis. Indeed, they came so fast that an increasing part of Mr Scarfell's job became the manipulation of his policy statements to match those used by the Ministry of Education, in order that the work of his staff would be as unaffected as possible. He was trying to mitigate the disruption of his pupils' education from this blizzard of changing priorities.

Now, thanks to Mr Harding, he could no longer maintain order by use of exclusion. With no effective sanction to deal with difficult children, he decided it was time to take early retirement. But there was no-one to take his place. His deputy heads were unwilling to take on the task. Nelson Mandela High was not an exciting school and it was too small to attract ambitious candidates. There were no applicants for the job.

Mr Harding had heard Miss Hunter speak at a meeting. He recognised her as a teacher who shared his belief in an open liberal approach. Children who misbehaved should be nurtured; their misdemeanours were not their fault. He called Miss Hunter to a meeting and asked her to apply for the job of head teacher.

Miss Hunter did not feel up to the task; she was aware that she lacked the qualities required to run the school. But Mr Harding was skilled in the art of persuasion. She agreed to give it a try on an acting basis and, after Mr Scarfell had been given a rousing cheer by the school assembly, she was on her own.

She quickly found herself out of her depth. She had managed to keep order in the classroom but it was different in the head teacher's study. After she had been sworn at for the third time in as many days by boys sent to see her for being disruptive in class, she began to suspect that her classroom control had been built on foundations provided by Mr Scarfell.

Little by little, she noticed changes in the school. The corridors and classrooms were noisier, there was more litter in the playground, children began wearing unauthorised variations of the school uniform, girls began wearing more make-up, and absenteeism was on the rise. At the same time, several teachers began sneaking off the school premises to smoke.

Miss Hunter's instinct that she was not up to the job was right. But the previously-unctuous Mr Harding was not prepared to help. His attentiveness had faded; he was brusque and dismissive when she contacted him for advice.

Her main task was dealing with children who had been rude to teachers. Reprimands failed and it was permutations of the same group of pupils who sat in a row outside her office day after day. She realised she was in real trouble when she was confronted with a girl who had spat in a teacher's face. She tried to coax the girl into explaining herself.

'So what's your problem?' shouted the girl, leaning over Miss Hunter's desk. 'What you gonna do? You want some too?'

Miss Hunter could find no words to reply. It was only the ghost of Mr Scarfell, still hovering in the room, that protected her from a gob of spit.

Miss Hunter suspended that girl for a week. But she realised that was no punishment. The girl, who had a patchy attendance record, was delighted to have time off school to do some daytime shoplifting

. . .

Kylie Wilson was fourteen. She had lost her mother when she was three years old and had been brought up by her father and elderly grandmother. This arrangement worked well until her grandmother died soon after Kylie started at Nelson Mandela School. Her father was a ticket clerk at the railway station. He worked shifts, so Kylie was accustomed to looking after herself when she came home from school.

She worked hard at school. She kept her bedroom tidy and, as she grew older, she helped with household chores and did some shopping on her way home. She and her father had settled into a comfortable routine, so Mr Wilson was puzzled when Kylie began to appear withdrawn. He guessed it must be her age. He was not one to push; he just hoped she would grow out of it.

It was not her age. Kylie was in trouble. Her best friend had dropped her, attaching herself instead to three girls who were taking advantage of the lax conditions at the school; they shortened their skirts and wore increasing quantities of black eye make-up. Kylie was spending her days alone, at the same time enduring snide remarks about her appearance. Soon the new gang of four were picking on her at every opportunity. When she met them in the corridor, they would spread themselves across the space so Kylie could not get past without jostling.

The cruelty of their remarks escalated. What was it like living alone with her Dad? How did she get on with the pervert? Had he done away with her Mum and Gran so he could have her to himself? Denial was pointless. Kylie was unable to tell her father because he would lose his temper. He was a kind man but he had a short fuse. There was no teacher she could turn to and her erstwhile best friend had become one of her tormentors. Even at home, there was no peace. Texts would appear on her mobile phone: 'Send our love to the pedo!'

She started to bunk off school. It was easy on the days her father was working because she could stay at home. On

27

other days, she drifted around the shopping arcade keeping a low profile. Soon Mr Wilson received a letter calling him in for a meeting. Miss Hunter was sympathetic but firm. She understood that he was a lone father of a teenage girl. It was hard for him but something had to be done. She suggested that he talk to Kylie that evening and Miss Hunter would see them both in the morning.

Mr Wilson confronted his daughter. And as he explained how disappointed he was, she started to weep inconsolably. He tried to comfort her but she pushed him away, so he sat and watched as she cried herself out. She said nothing. Later that evening, he told her about the meeting with Miss Hunter next morning.

The meeting was awkward. Kylie mumbled when asked questions and neither Miss Hunter nor Mr Wilson could extract anything from her.

'Why don't I leave the two of you alone?' said Mr Wilson when he realised he had nothing to contribute.

Miss Hunter had a warm personality which came into its own when dealing with a child in distress. It took some time but she coaxed Kylie into telling her about the bullying and to give the names of her tormentors.

The four girls were not among the 'usual suspects', so Miss Hunter thought she could nip the problem in the bud. She called the girls into her study. They smirked when she told them to be kind to a girl who had lost her mother and grandmother. She spoke to them about friendship and loyalty, but they were still smirking as they filed out of her study

. . .

A dinner lady in Nelson Mandela School lived in the same street as the Wilsons. She did not know the family but would say hello when she passed Mr Wilson in the street. And seeing him two days after his meeting with Miss Hunter, she asked him whether Kylie was feeling better.

'She's alright, I think,' he replied. 'Why do you ask?'

'Hasn't she told you about the fight?'

'No, she hasn't. What happened?'

The dinner lady described how four girls had cornered Kylie outside the toilets, snatched her shoulder bag and began beating her with it. It was only the intervention of a male teacher that prevented Kylie being seriously hurt.

A few minutes later, Miss Hunter received a telephone call from Mr Wilson. She told him she was very sorry about the incident and was dealing with it. She then rang Mr Harding and insisted on a meeting. She got his attention when she told him she intended to exclude four girls from the school.

At the meeting, Miss Hunter explained what had happened and said she could see no alternative to excluding the four girls. Mr Harding was annoyed at the prospect of losing his cherished position in the school-exclusion rankings. Miss Hunter had seen him wheedle and cajole to get his own way, and now she saw how angry he could be when thwarted. He spoke to her in slow, measured tones.

'Listen,' he said. 'You will do three things. First, launch an investigation into how the incident was dealt with. If your member of staff touched any of the girls when breaking up the fight, I want to know. I will deal with him. Second, send an official warning to the dinner lady. If she breaks a confidence again about a pupil, she will be dismissed. Third, explain to Mr Wilson that, as his daughter is a truant, she is clearly not settling at Nelson Mandela. It would be to all our benefits if he moved her to another school.'

Miss Hunter was overwhelmed by the power of his personality. She felt unable to stand up for herself, to counter this barrage of instruction. She returned to the school, sent an official warning letter to the dinner lady, and arranged a meeting with Mr Wilson the following day.

. . .

Next morning, Mr Wilson met the dinner lady outside his front door, her finger poised to ring the bell. She showed him her official warning from Miss Hunter.

So it was that, Mr Wilson arrived at the school in a state of rage. When Miss Hunter suggested that he might like to find a new school for Kylie, he exploded – an outburst of violence for which Miss Hunter could not find it in her heart to blame him.

And so it was that, as she sat on the hospital trolley, she refused to make a statement to the police.

The Man who Stole Bryce Canyon

In which the GREEDY defend the fruits they pluck from the trees

You're the most beautiful thing I've ever seen,' he said. 'You're even more beautiful than Bryce Canyon.'

Tom guided Emily across the dance floor. Physically they were close but he knew they were separated by a huge social gulf. He chose his words carefully.

'I beg your pardon,' said Emily, taken aback by this unexpected chat-up line.

'Bryce Canyon. It's in the bottom right hand corner of Utah. It's actually the edge of a red sandstone cliff, not a canyon at all. But the rock's been worn away to form a forest of fingers and thumbs all pointing skywards. They're different shapes and sizes. Some look like castles, others like mythical creatures. There are thousands upon thousands of them. The Indians call them hoodoos.'

'It sounds wonderful.'

'But that's only the beginning. Twice a day, at dawn and dusk, when the sun is behind them, the hoodoos seem to catch fire. It's hard to describe. The light bounces off one layer and illuminates the back of another. With each repeated reflection, the colour changes from one shade of red to another. Sometimes there's an orange tinge, at others there are myriad shades of pink. The rock seems to glow.'

'Oh my,' said Emily, melting into his arms.

'I'd love to share it with you,' said Tom. Emily's eyes told him that he was more than halfway there.

. . .

Tom had worked hard to reach the point where he could even dare to ask Emily to dance. But this was just one milestone on the long road he had mapped out for himself when he was

31

a boy.

His father was a doctor in a desert community in south-eastern New Mexico. It was the time of the Great Depression when people were finding it hard to pay their bills. Tom's father once accepted an old Model T Ford Sedan in lieu of payment.

He took advantage of this and, a few months later, he organised a vacation in Arizona and Utah to see the high plateau and the canyons. Tom pressed his nose to the car window as they set off through New Mexico. Not far from home, he saw a strange wooden structure, a criss-cross of beams forming a small tower.

'What's that, Pa?'

'An oil derrick. You won't see many around here.'

'Why not?'

'All the oil is east of here, in Texas. They have thousands of derricks there and some people have become enormously rich. There's almost no oil here, so we're dirt poor.'

That's unfair, thought Tom.

Their first destination was the Grand Canyon which was more than two miles wide. Tom felt that he was looking at a painting on an immense canvas, a painting in which the colours were constantly changing. The plan was to spend the night in a cabin at the canyon's edge and move on next morning. But Tom wanted to take a mule ride down the canyon side. His mother did not like mules, so he grabbed the advantage.

'You wouldn't mind if Pa and I went down into the canyon tomorrow?' he asked his mother. 'You could rest up here.'

'You boys go and have a good time,' she replied.

They set off next morning down the Bright Angel Path and Tom was awestruck by the wonderland he was riding through. After another night in the cabin, the tour continued as Tom and his parents travelled from one marvel to another. They saw Monument Valley, Canyon de Cheilly, Zion, and Arches. Bryce Canyon was the last. Tom's father knew it would be the best.

They stayed at Ruby's Inn, decades before tourist coaches would arrive to fill the canyon with a never-ending stream of people. But even then, it was almost impossible to enjoy a viewpoint alone.

'Wouldn't it be great to have this to ourselves?' said Tom's father as they watched the setting sun turn the sculpted pillars into a furnace of flaming spires.

Yes, thought Tom. And that night he dreamt that one day he would own Bryce Canyon and keep it to himself.

. . .

Shortly after their return from the canyon, his father asked Tom to exercise the pony.

'I've the car now,' he said, 'and we don't want the pony to be idle.'

Tom had often walked for miles on foot, but now he could go much further. Billy, his best friend at school, was a rancher's son whose father owned a vast tract of land which barely sustained a small herd of cattle. Billy's father was happy for Tom to explore his land and he soon knew almost every ridge and gully.

One day, Tom noticed a black shiny seepage oozing from the ground. He dismounted, tied the pony to a Joshua tree that grew tight against a boulder, and found a smooth rock shaped like a bench. Perhaps, he thought, it had been put there especially for him to sit and contemplate this small pool of oil. He settled himself on the stone and glanced at a patch of scrub close by. Coiled and motionless, a rattlesnake lay warming itself in the sun. Tom saw the triangular shape of its head wrapped in its coils. He was not afraid. He just sat very still and watched the snake in the bright light of the hot afternoon.

He sat very still as his gaze moved between the patterns on the snake's back and the pool of black oil, its smooth dark surface reflecting the rays of the sun. The snake, the oil, the heat, the Joshua tree – a rare sight in that part of New Mexico – all came together. And in that moment, Tom was changed for ever.

He had always been a good boy and it came as a shock

when he started to think differently. Perhaps it was the snake which tempted him, a creature whose role in life was to hypnotise victims before striking them down with venomous fangs. Perhaps it was the hot sun which could desiccate any living being. Perhaps it was the tangled arms of the Joshua tree which moved the needle on his moral compass. For two thoughts came into Tom's mind, as if from nowhere.

The first was: If it's alright for folks in Texas to be rich because they live on a great pond of oil, why shouldn't I get rich too? I'm smarter than most of them.

And then: Everyone looks after themselves. If they stop me taking what I want, I'll walk away. But what they allow me to take will belong to me. Finders keepers.

As these thoughts came into his mind, the pony noticed the snake. It reared and whinnied as the snake uncoiled itself and slid away under the bush. And when Tom returned home, he put the first part of his plan into operation. He said nothing about his find and he was careful not to return to the same place on the rancher's land. The oil was his secret

Tom had a talent to bend and twist people to his will. He could do this in a gentle and almost imperceptible way. This was how he made his father agree to take the mule ride into the Grand Canyon. A year or so later, as part two of his plan, he decided to turn his friend Billy against his older brother Jake. His chance came on Jake's seventeenth birthday when his father, Jethro Moss, gave him a palomino stallion as a birthday present.

'It's time for you to help on the ranch,' he said.

'That's a great horse,' Tom said to Billy a few days later. 'Guess your Pa don't think you deserve a horse like that?'

Jake was proud of his horse. He showed it off to Samantha Nole, the town beauty, and they soon became sweethearts.

'Don't you wish it was you?' said Tom to Billy. 'He's only got her because of the stallion.'

There was a fight a few days later when Jake was thrown

off while trying to break a mustang. Conscious of his loss of dignity, he was furious when Billy burst out laughing. He picked himself up, vaulted the fence and landed a fist on his brother's jaw. When Tom heard the news, he came to the ranch to sympathise.

'Jake gets away with murder,' he said. 'Just last week he left ten cattle up on that ridge and your Pa said nothing.'

The brothers soon began to fight more frequently and Jethro, who loved them both, began to rethink his plan to pass the land to them in joint ownership. Tom, meanwhile, was being as helpful as he could on the ranch.

'I seen a bunch of your cattle over by Bolger's land,' he said to Jethro one day. 'You want me to drive them back over this way next time I'm up there?'

'That would be a kindness.'

'How many head are you sellin' next month? I hear prices are real good right now.'

'Can't say good, but a sight better than a year ago. It's a good time to sell, I reckon. No rain and the creeks are near dry.'

'Can I come with you to market?' Tom asked. 'I've never been.'

'Sure. It'll be a pleasure.'

. . .

Another year or so later, Tom received a legacy from an aunt. He was ready for part three of his plan. He waited for the right time to make his move, which came when the brothers had a fist-fight in the yard after Billy made a crude comment about Samantha and the stallion. By the time Jethro heard the commotion, both boys had bloody faces and Billy had lost two teeth. Next day, Tom went to see Jethro.

'I heard about the fight yesterday,' he said.

'I dunno what to do,' said Jethro. 'I wanna stop working the ranch but it won't be safe with them two at each other's throats.'

'Well,' said Tom, 'you know how it is when you're old

enough to drink. Some just can't hold their liquor.'

'And how can I leave the ranch to them if they're gonna drink and fight?'

Tom timed his next remark carefully.

'How would it be,' he asked, 'if you sold the ranch and shared the money?'

'I guess that might work.'

'I just heard,' Tom continued, hoping that Jethro would be too upset to notice his lack of subtlety, 'that my aunt Martha has left me $3000 in her will. I know your ranch is worth more than that, but it's all I can afford right now. And I'll give you half what I get for the first hundred cattle I sell.'

'I thought you was gonna follow your Pa and be a doc.'

'No. I like the outdoors too much. And I'm not one for books.'

'What'll I do with Jake and Billy?' Jethro wondered aloud, not expecting a reply.

'Billy and Jake don't get on,' said Tom, having carefully prepared his answer. 'Leaving the ranch to them is only going to make things worse. They're gonna fight and you'll be lucky if they don't kill each other. I don't suppose they'd say no to a stack of money.'

'You could be right.'

'I'm sure I could make a go of it. Sell the ranch to me and share out the money between them. Then they can't say you've favoured one over the other.'

Jethro accepted the offer, low though it was. It solved the problem of his sons and the ranch would belong to a young man who would take good care of it

. . .

Tom knew that he would have to be immensely rich to make his dream of Bryce Canyon come true. One oil well would not be enough. Having obtained the ranch on the cheap from a disappointed old man, he would have to plan more carefully in the future. His victims must walk away unaware of what had happened to them.

36

He had guessed that the oil fields of western Texas extended into the south-east corner of New Mexico. Before any mention was made of his find, he had to make sure that everyone knew that prospecting was an expensive business.

'Oil,' he said to anyone who would listen. 'It's ruined many a man who's been sucked in but found nothing.'

Over the next few years, he made deals with local ranchers, offering to pay to prospect their land in exchange for a perpetual share in any finds made. Only then did a prospecting team arrive on his property. They found a lot of oil. And oil was found on his neighbours' land too.

The plan had worked. Tom was rich. And before long he owned oilfields stretching from Texas to California

. . .

A few years later, Tom returned to New Mexico to see his father who was dying of cancer.

'Listen son,' the old man said, 'You're making your way in the world. You're doing well. I'm proud of you. But a father worries. I'll be gone soon. I've provided for your mother, so you've no worries there. But you need to look after yourself.'

'Why fret, Pa?' asked Tom. He guessed what might be coming but his father's reply surprised him.

'You've made a pile of money and it looks like you'll make a whole lot more. Now you remember the things that money can't buy. It can't buy friendship, or health, or love. It also can't buy time. However much you possess, you only have one life. What good are things if they sit locked away gathering dust?'

Tom felt he had been let off lightly. He had cheated and been successful. He had been dishonest and turned his lies into profit. He had courted the friendship of his neighbours and abused their trust. And all his father had to say was that he would not have time to enjoy the fruits of his success. But he sometimes felt uncomfortable. Every time he bought himself something new and expensive, he could feel his shoulders tensing with a twinge of guilt. Self-indulgence did not come easily.

One afternoon he found himself in Dallas. His business day was over and, instead of returning to the hotel, he went shopping. Still a cowboy at heart, riding into town with money to burn, he decided to buy himself some boots.

He found an expensive boot-maker's store, drew himself up to his full height and walked in. The room was dusty and smelled of leather.

'I want the dandyiest pair of boots you can make.'

'So you'll be wanting snakeskin,' said the boot-maker.

Tom remembered the rattlesnake and the Joshua tree.

'I guess I will,' he said.

Most of the boots in the shop were working boots, but there was one pair made of fine hide with tall heels and pointed toes.

'Can you make me a pair like those?'

'Sure can. How high d'you want the heels?'

'Taller than those,' said Tom, aware that tall men made a good impression. 'And in snakeskin if you please.'

He imagined himself standing a little taller. He saw himself at his next meeting, in a plush hotel armchair with his legs stretched out, crossing his feet from time to time to draw attention to his smart new boots.

. . .

Although the oil price rose and fell over the years, Tom's empire grew so large that he had no need to worry. High oil prices increased his profits; low oil prices gave him opportunities to buy more wells. With wells in seventeen states and an interest in a refinery, Tom was an oil magnate.

By the time he decided to buy a mansion, his qualms about spending had faded. He wanted a house to impress. He had to climb the social ladder to make his dream come true. He picked Houston for his new home. It was close to the Gulf of Mexico and it was home to the rich and powerful. And so he would not look like an upstart hick, he hired a well-known, expensive architect.

'Where should I build to make the best impression?' was

his first question.

The architect thought for a moment.

'South of the city,' he said. 'There are good areas on Clear Lake. You can build a house overlooking the lake and you can keep a boat. There's nothing that makes a better impression than a party on the water.'

'Oh, yes,' said Tom. 'I like the idea of that.'

'And the land around the house can be landscaped with woods and gardens.'

Tom thought of green lawns, very different from the yuccas, cactus and tumbleweed of his youth. He wanted the new house to be special.

'You build me a place that everyone will wish they had,' he said. 'You build me a place that'll go down in history.'

The architect's design resembled a Venetian palazzo with balconies overlooking the water. It would have been easy to design a pastiche, but the architect had a good sense of style and Tom had the money to indulge his vision. There would be imported marble, hand-sculpted carvings, the finest wrought iron. Everything would be the best that money could buy.

'I want to do something different inside the house,' said the architect. 'I want to go for the latest style. Art Deco. It's all the rage back East. How about stone reliefs on the walls illustrating the oil industry?'

Tom often came to Clear Lake to see the progress on the house. He watched craftsmen carve Art Deco plaques and delivery men unpack vanloads of gleaming chrome furniture. Scenes of activity morphed into suites of calm, graceful rooms.

And when he finally moved into the house of his dreams, his snakeskin boots found a place in a closet and were never worn again

. . .

Tom's parties were legendary in Texas. He was accepted by the oil men as one of their own. But this was not enough. For Bryce Canyon belonged to the nation; money alone would not

39

realise his dream.

In the years that followed, he moved his centre of operations to the east coast, buying another mansion in the Hamptons on Long Island where he could rub shoulders with the powerful. And then he bought a villa in the Caribbean. And to make the most of that, he bought a private plane. This was part of a new phase in his plan. He had realised his teenage ambition for money; now, still in his thirties, he began to court power. And for this he needed a suitable wife.

Emily was the daughter of a top lawyer in Boston, a grandee of the Republican Party, whose firm handled Tom's business dealings. He set himself the task of winning her hand. He knew this would not be easy. Despite his wealth, he still the butt of class prejudice but soon Robert Fisher, Emily's father, began to notice that he was not merely a 'hick from the boon docks'. One summer, he invited Tom to a ball in his mansion. And Tom did not flunk the opportunity.

It was a short courtship and, after the wedding Tom was welcomed into society. He had also gained a father-in-law who could teach him how to play the political game.

. . .

While Emily spent money refurbishing his houses, Tom ordered a 325-foot yacht with seventeen staterooms. He named her *The Bryce Canyon* and kept her in the Caribbean, manned with a permanent crew and ready to sail at short notice.

Shortly after his marriage, Tom began to understand his father's final words. In the early days of his wealth, he had enjoyed the freedom of having plenty of money. He bought whatever took his fancy, mostly from specialist shops which stocked 'exclusive items' at very high prices. But now he realised that he did not have the time to enjoy his yacht and his houses, all the things his wealth had brought him. At the same time, Robert was teaching him another lesson.

'You know, my boy,' he said over brandy and cigars on the deck of *The Bryce Canyon*, 'you should be careful about flaunting your wealth. Envy is a dangerous thing.'

'So what should I do?'

'You can either cut yourself off. Build walls and fences round your houses. Have nothing to do with the rest of the world. Or you can throw money into good works. Emily can help with that. She'd love to spend your money being patron to half a dozen charities. She could show off designer dresses at charity balls and dinners. And you could give speeches saying how important it is to look after those who are less fortunate. The public will love you for it.'

So Tom and Emily gave large sums of money to charity, which did little to diminish their wealth. Tom ensured that his donations were well publicised, while a small army of accountants and lawyers ensured that he paid very little tax.

. . .

In the third year of their marriage, Emily gave birth to her first and only child. After an uneventful pregnancy, her son John was introduced to the press corps a few days after his birth. His progress through an idyllic childhood filled pages in the gossip columns and consolidated his parents' reputation as a model family. Robert was closely involved in his grandson's upbringing. He ensured that he was baptised and received a religious education. Tom was not a religious man but his protests were overruled.

'A boy like yours,' Robert explained, 'with wealth and position, may want to go into politics. You wouldn't deny him that opportunity?'

'Of course not.'

'To succeed in politics in these great United States, a man must be seen to fear God. It doesn't matter whether he believes or not, he must talk the talk. However questionable his politics, with a religious background he can always claim the moral high ground.'

. . .

Soon after John's fourteenth birthday, his father told him of his childhood visit to Arizona and Utah. He told him every detail he could remember about the canyons. He told him of his dream of owning Bryce Canyon and was delighted to see an answering glint in John's eyes.

'I've worked hard to make the dream come true,' said

41

Tom. 'But it may not happen in my lifetime. I hope that you, my son, will carry on the cause. If it was simply a matter of money, we'd have it by now. But the state won't sell. So we must watch and wait. We must be in the right place at the right time. And we must make sure – when the opportunity comes – that the law is on our side. You've got my money and your mother's blood. Come with me to Bryce Canyon. Then decide whether you want to pick up the baton. But tell no one about our dream.'

A few days later, as the sun dropped low in the sky, John stood on the rim of the canyon and watched the colour of the hoodoos melt and change and flare into bright oranges and reds. His cheeks burned as he watched and he took his father's hand.

'Let's do it,' he said.

. . .

John was close to his grandfather Robert. They spent time together and often discussed politics, one of Robert's favourite subjects.

'Democracy is all well and good,' said Robert one afternoon during the school summer holiday, 'but most voters are ignorant. They always were. They always will be. You can't count on them to see what's staring them in the face. They're easily led. And the socialists always try to get the upper hand. We can't let them get away with it, John. They'll tax us out of existence. Democracy will be dead and that'll be the end of the American Dream.'

'No contradiction in that?' asked John.

'No,' said Robert. 'Democracy is about freedom. And we can't let anything get in the way of our freedom to make this nation great.'

John had never been a spoilt child, but he did feel a sense of entitlement. Poor people, he thought, should be provided with charitable condescension, not helped out of poverty. As he grew up, he decided that he would be a puller of strings rather than an active politician. And when he took over the reins of business from his father, he began to make political donations, mostly to the Republican Party but also to a few selected Democrats.

He also expanded the business abroad. He had a well-hidden contempt for those less privileged than himself and, with most of the world's oil found in countries ruled by unsavoury leaders, he was happy to deal face-to-face with despots. To obtain the best possible access to the oil, he opened a publishing house with a single specialisation: autobiographies of the men whom he wished to flatter. These men could either write their own stories with the help of a ghost writer, or the publishing house would commission a hagiography. There were very few sales to the public but John set up companies to buy the books in bulk, providing their subjects with eye-watering royalty statements.

And now he was given an unexpected bonus. Arab dissidents, who hated their leaders and resented their links to the West, widened their struggle and began to operate on the international stage. When a massive atrocity was carried out on American soil, John called in favours from the politicians he had supported so generously. He nudged his friends in high places to strengthen anti-terrorist laws and restrict freedoms in order 'to protect the homeland'.

These measures were passed into law. At the same time, Tom and Emily were acting as philanthropic heart-throbs to the nation. Their images appeared on the covers of magazines, they attended glittering functions, and they poured money into charitable donations.

. . .

When the time came to marry, John chose his wife as well as his father had done: Angeline was the willowy daughter of an investment banker. This gave him an opportunity to learn about the intricacies of banking from Arthur Goodman, his new father-in-law. He brought up the subject one evening after dinner in the Clear Lake mansion.

'My father grew up in New Mexico,' he said. 'People had very little back then. They did not trust banks. They kept their money under their bed or anywhere else the bankers couldn't get it. Banks want to lend you money when things go well. But if there's no rain and you need money, if you really need money, then it's no dice. It seems that the banks get

43

richer and the people get poorer.'

'That's so in a way,' said Arthur. 'But it's complicated.'

John refilled their wine glasses. 'So tell me,' he said.

'Okay. I'll start with retail banks, the ordinary banks in the main streets of towns and cities. They hold the money which people need to live their lives. If they fail, catastrophe follows as surely as day follows night.'

'How's that?'

'People's savings vanish. They can't pay their bills. The people they owe get nothing. A ball starts to roll. And it's a bad, bad ball. Other banks are wiped out. People rely on each other to pay their debts – and so do the banks. When this ball starts to roll, people can't repay their loans and, even if a bank has collateral, who's going to buy foreclosed land when no-one has money? Another bank fails and soon there are more victims and more repossessions and the government is caught between a rock and a hard place. They can either bail out the banks or they're stuck with an economic calamity. So they bail out the banks.'

'Is that why banks are so tough about lending money?'

'It is. The government doesn't want to bail them out, so it makes rules about how much money banks can lend and who they can lend it to. It's the only way they can avoid being stuck with the bill.'

'So where's the problem?'

'It's the investment banks. Like my bank. They're different. Their money comes from rich people who want to make the most of their money. These people can afford to take risks. But they want higher rates of interest in exchange for taking these risks. The Holy Grail for an investment bank is to merge with a retail bank. That gives it access to a huge amount of cheap money, the cash that ordinary people deposit on low interest rates because they believe there's no risk. When an investment bank lends this money out at high interest rates, or it speculates with it, then it can make a fortune. Unfortunately, there've been rules against that since the last crash. They no longer allow investment banks to hook up with the retail ones.'

Arthur emptied his wine glass and held it out for a refill.

'Even if it was allowed,' he continued after John had poured the wine, 'there's the problem of finding enough people to lend the money to. One way is to relax the rules. You lend the money to people with no collateral and they pay through the nose for the privilege. But the best way is to get an asset-price bubble going.'

'What on earth is that?'

'Imagine you own a bank stuffed full of money on which you pay low rates of interest. You persuade people to borrow this money from you at much higher rates of interest. To buy houses for example. That sets a different ball rolling. You're lending money to people who want to buy their own homes, people who've never had the chance of borrowing that kind of money before. They go out with their loans and bid for the houses that are there. And because there's all this new money and no new houses, the house prices go up. And when the prices go up, other people don't want to get left out. So they borrow more money to buy more houses. Soon you have every man and his dog knocking at your door asking to borrow money. And because you've paid next to nothing for the money you lend them, your profits get larger and larger.'

'A bit like making cotton candy,' said John. 'You start off with a bit of sugar and you spin and spin it into an enormous cloud.'

'Just like that. Sweet.'

'And when prices stop going up because people can't pay back what they owe, the whole thing deflates?'

'It's best not to think about that. You make hay while the sun shines. You're a farm boy at heart. That should make good sense to you.'

'So, making it easier for investment and retail banks to get together would be good for you?'

'You bet it would.'

Later that evening, As John strolled along the foreshore of Clear Lake, an idea formed in his mind: *I wonder what it would take to bring the Federal Reserve to the brink of bankruptcy.*

He began to call in political favours. Soon politicians were saying: 'These regulations are hindering the operation of the free market These guys know what they are doing, they can regulate themselves ... Government only ever gets it wrong.' And slowly but surely the government relaxed the banking rules. Soon Arthur's bank was able to merge with a retail bank, making vast profits as it lent increasing sums of money to risky ventures.

. . .

John spent the next few years consolidating his position. He continued to make money and he added to his circle of powerful friends. His parents grew older, more venerable, more venerated. Arthur's bank continued to grow in size and wealth, taking every opportunity available as the banking regulations were relaxed.

Like his father before him, he and Angeline had just one child, Stephen, a boy who was cast in the family mould – smart, forward thinking and arrogant. When he began his studies at Yale, his grandfather took him to one side and told him of his dream. Stephen was intrigued. Perhaps, he thought, he would be the one to finally realise the dream.

Although they were less comfortable in the role of philanthropists, John and Angeline took on the mantle that Tom and Emily were now too old to wear. And soon the business passed into Stephen's capable hands. He was careful not to invest in Arthur's bank but, when the bubble burst and banks began to fail, he was waiting in the wings to lend a helping hand.

This was the calamity he had been hoping for, a calamity which forced the government to bail-out the banking sector. Stephen waited long enough to ensure there was real economic damage, until people were too concerned about their own finances to understand the implications of a bail-out. His political friends swung into action, the rescue measures were announced, and a large stimulus package was put in place to ensure 'a robust future'.

People lost their jobs, businesses failed, mortgage

payments were missed, and foreclosures devastated asset prices throughout the world. The weakest suffered most but well-educated people with highly-paid jobs were also affected. With so much suffering, there was little opposition to the government pouring yet more money into the banking sector. But its coffers were empty – failed businesses and the unemployed paid no tax – so it was forced to borrow huge sums of money. The Federal Reserve was brought to the brink of bankruptcy.

As the dust settled, business started to pick up again, and the government thought about how to repay its debts. They increased taxes and cut welfare. Public services deteriorated as government employees lost their jobs. Then they thought of privatisation. Why not sell government property? That was when a junior Congressman came up with an idea.

'Why don't we sell the National Parks?' he said.

Supporters of the scheme insisted that buyers would keep the parks open to the public. They would need to make money, they said. They would be helped by generous tax breaks. But opposition was fierce. When some of the protests turned to violence, the President invoked the homeland security powers which had been enacted after the terrorist attacks. Tear gas was deployed on the streets, demonstrators were arrested, protests were squashed.

Stephen was the first to bid for Bryce Canyon after the proposal was passed. His bid was slightly higher than the next best offer. He had the best of connections. After the formalities had been arranged, the family put their signatures to a larger money transfer than any of them had ever made. A few weeks later, a team of workmen arrived at the canyon. They installed high steel barriers around the perimeter with large signs with red letters reading PRIVATE PROPERTY. KEEP OUT.

Tom could die happy. And John and Stephen had one more property in their portfolio. They visited Bryce Canyon from time to time, about once every two years. And when they did, they had it to themselves.

In which the SLOTH of authority bears down on the innocent

'Do I look black to you?' asked Brian.

Two men were facing each other at a Formica table in the police canteen. Each had a steaming mug of tea and two chocolate digestive biscuits wrapped in cellophane. Brian had just finished his first shift in the station.

Bill was embarrassed by the question, but he had a reputation for plain speaking. He looked carefully at Brian. The hair was black and curly. The eyes were dark brown. The lips were large and on the grey side of pink.

'I'd say you've got some black features. But it's not the first thing I'd have noticed.'

'That's what I told the chief constable. If you want someone who looks black, I said, you want my sister. She's got Afro hair, though her skin is only pale coffee. She runs a sales team for a drugs company. But as I told him, the police couldn't match her salary. He insisted though, because he wants people like me to rise up through the ranks. People like me! I ask you! I'm the original PC Plod. I was happy walking the beat. Keeping my nose clean.'

'So why did he choose you?' asked Bill.

'It's the racial minorities thing. That riot in London and the police accused of institutional racism. The word went out for chief constables to promote racial minorities.'

'I remember.'

'But we never saw ourselves as a racial minority. My Gran was from Jamaica, but there was white blood and my Mum wasn't dark. My Granddad was a merchant seaman. He met my Gran in Kingston and brought her back here. It was a surprise when my sister came out with Afro hair. We just thought we were like everyone else. My sister did well at school, went to university. I was the dumb one.'

Bill munched one of his biscuits. 'So what did the chief constable do?'

'He told me to apply for the sergeant's exam. That'll be a waste of time, I said. But he wouldn't listen. "You just do it, lad. Let me worry about the rest." I don't know how he managed it but I passed. You should've seen the fanfare. I got wheeled out in front of the press – with the chief constable beside me. "We're proud to announce the appointment of the first sergeant from a minority group," he said. I could see them, the journalists, looking at me a bit strange, but they print what they're told. And the extra money came in handy.'

'So what went wrong?' asked Brian. "Why were you transferred here?'

'Like I told him, I wasn't up to it. My arrest record was bad. My conviction rate was worse. My squad could see that I didn't have what it took. It wasn't long before they disintegrated. It was a shambles.'

'You really couldn't get it together? Did things get better?'

'It was just when they were bringing in targets. We were nowhere close to them, so I got hauled in to the chief constable. It was his own fault but he wasn't giving up. He sent me on courses – motivation, man management, time management, every sort of bloody management. I just didn't get it.'

. . .

The chief constable sat behind a mahogany desk and nibbled on a Jaffa cake. His secretary had brought it with his coffee, served on the silver tray presented to him by local shopkeepers who were grateful for a more visible police presence. He had just finished a telephone conversation. The news was good. As he had done several times before, he had extricated himself from a difficult situation.

He had navigated his career by following the line of least resistance. And his great talent was to spot the easiest way of achieving his goals. Many chief constables had reacted badly to the introduction of targets, but he revelled in them.

'Life is easier if you have a target that can be achieved by ticking the right boxes,' he told his staff. 'You just have to know what falls inside the boxes and what falls outside. Then you make sure you can tick the boxes and Bob's your uncle.'

Before the target culture was imposed, he had used his principle of least effort to deal with another problem. This had not been a success – and his recent telephone conversation was the end of a long story that began when he made another of his easy decisions.

The police had been criticised for the heavy-handed way in which they dealt with a race riot in London. Soon afterwards, a black teenager had been beaten to death in a gang battle over drugs. The black community, already bruised, was incensed by a series of dawn raids. They refused to co-operate, so the police were unable to hold suspects for lack of evidence.

In the panic that followed, a scheme of positive discrimination was implemented. The idea was to recruit more policemen from racial minorities and fast-track their careers. In this way, the police force would 'more closely reflect the diversity of communities it serves'. This was just up the chief constable's street. It allowed him, with little effort, to stand out among his peers.

He determined to be one of the first chief constables to have a black inspector. This would, he thought, be easy because he had been told of a black constable in his force. It was disappointing to learn that the black constable only had a mediocre record, but the colour of his skin would surely make up for this. But he was taken aback when he called Brian in to his office: the man hardly looked black at all.

'How does your family find life in England?' he began, awkwardly.

Brain looked puzzled. 'Much the same as anyone else, I suppose.'

'I thought you came from the Caribbean.'

'Only my Gran.'

'Oh,' said the chief constable, unaccustomed to having the wind taken out of his sails.

51

He persevered, persuading Brian to apply for the sergeant's examination and telling him that he would arrange some coaching. Brian tried to explain that this would be an uphill struggle – but the chief constable refused to listen.

A few weeks later, when the officer coaching Brian submitted a discouraging report, the chief constable pulled a few strings. Brian scraped through the examination and was promoted to sergeant. He did not do well in his new role. The chief constable did his best to help but nothing worked – except for the last course that Brian attended, a two-day seminar titled 'Making Targets Work'.

This Brian found easy to grasp. With arrest targets, there was no difference between arresting people for minor offences and arresting them for major crimes. With conviction targets, there was no difference between offences that were easy to prove and offences that required the careful accumulation of evidence. An arrest was an arrest. A conviction was a conviction.

The lecturer spelt it out. "People who've had no contact with the law have little or no experience of dealing with the police. They don't have the skills that criminals use to avoid arrest. They are so much easier to catch. And because they aren't as slippery as habitual criminals, they are also easier to convict."

Brian understood this. After he explained it to his team of constables, there was an immediate improvement in their conviction rate. The convictions were mostly for dropping litter, failing to keep dogs under control, drunk and disorderly behaviour, driving without a seat-belt, eating while driving, broken car lights, and a range of minor motoring offences. And Brian sent his constables into villages with hand-held speed cameras and obtained even more convictions.

. . .

Two men sat at a trestle table in the community centre of the market town. They ate Jammie Dodgers and sipped tea out of chunky earthenware mugs.

'You won't be able to start till your CRB check has come through' said Joe. 'It'll take several months but, as soon as it comes, we'll be delighted to have your help.'

'Thanks,' said Nick. He was volunteering to help in the club for disaffected youth which had recently opened in response to the gang brawls that broke out most Saturday nights. 'I'll look forward to it.'

'These checks are a bloody nuisance. The Criminal Records Bureau, it's called. I just don't understand. The police know when someone's a risk to kids – but they don't tell anyone about it, even when they're asked. Then you get a tragedy when a kid is killed and, by some twisted logic, we're all guilty till proved innocent. I've heard a little about what happened to you. You were acquitted and supposed to get an apology from the police?'

'That's right,' said Nick, his fingers stroking the mug of tea.

'Do you mind telling me about it?'

'It's a bit of a long story. Kelly, my wife, and I moved here two years ago. We live near the Ramsden Arms. It's a friendly neighbourhood and Kelly made friends with the old folk – she'd do their shopping for them. Then it started to get noisy at night. Rowdy kids would come down our way, shouting and throwing rubbish in the gardens. The old folk were frightened. You don't want to put up with that when you're elderly.'

'You certainly don't.'

'I rang the police but they were about as good as a chocolate teapot. We can't do anything unless a crime is committed, they said. I asked if it wasn't a crime to make noise and drop litter. Not a priority, they said. Things got worse after a few weeks. There was one old lady who couldn't stop crying on Saturday nights because it was so bad. Kelly would go and sit with her. And one night, a bottle was thrown through her window.'

'The police must have taken an interest then.'

'They sent a young constable who took a statement. He didn't hold out much hope. No evidence, he said. What about finger prints? asked the old lady, like on TV? And you know what the copper said? It costs too much for a minor crime, he said. It's not a priority. So that was that.'

'Makes you wonder what we pay the police for.'

'Anyway, the thing about not enough evidence got me thinking. So I bought a closed-circuit camera and hooked it up to my video recorder. It was tricky fixing the camera so it covered most of the street, but I managed in the end. It was a cheap thing and the pictures weren't great, but I asked the police to come and look at them. They told me not to waste their time. They said I might need a licence to operate it. They said I might be breaking the law.'

'That's hardly believable,' said Joe. 'After all that effort.'

'The next Saturday night, there was an almighty thump on the front door. Then another. I pulled the curtains back and there were five kids clustered round our gate. One of them chucked a brick into the garden. Kelly, who'd just come back from sitting with the old lady, phoned the police. Then a bottle came through the window. Kelly tried to stop me, but I thought I could reason with them. I'm a big bloke and they were just a bunch of kids. One of them had a stick. As I walked up to the gate, they began shouting at me.'

'I don't think I would have dared to do that.'

'You can't fault the speed of the police response. The car came round the corner just as I reached the gate and the kid with the stick took a swipe at me. I grabbed the stick and took it off him. Then the kids scarpered. The police didn't follow them. One of the coppers took the stick from me, while the other one talked to the station on his radio.

Nick took another mouthful of tea. 'They asked me what had happened, who had made the phone call, and what was I doing with the stick. I said I took it off one of the kids. They said they'd seen me wielding an offensive weapon. So they arrested me on suspicion of assault. Then they took the video out of the recorder and said it would be used as evidence against me.'

'Not good enough to catch the kids, but good enough to prosecute you.'

'I was cautioned, handcuffed, and taken down the station. Have you seen a police cell? Bare walls, a hard bench, concrete floor, and stainless steel toilet. When they close the door, after they've taken your belt and shoe laces and your dignity, you're all alone. It was late by this time and Kelly didn't know what to do. I spent the night in the cell before she got a lawyer to bail me out.'

'That must have been a relief,' said Joe.

'I could go home but I still had the assault charge hanging over me. The police used the video to identify the kid – which wasn't hard because he was "known to the police" as they say. They interviewed him, after which the charge became assaulting a minor. Then there were months of waiting. The lawyer told me not to worry, but I soon got depressed and began taking days off work. I didn't feel up to anything. And then I got the sack. Long story short, I ended up on tranquilisers and anti-depressants. Kelly was a brick – but what could she do?'

'I can't imagine how you must have felt,' said Joe, putting a consoling hand on Nick's arm. 'It's so unjust.'

'When the trial came up, it was a bit of an anti-climax. The police showed my video. One of the policeman said he'd seen me assault the boy, but they'd had him examined by a doctor who couldn't find any marks on him. The boy himself was surprisingly honest. He said he'd gone for me and that I took the stick away from him. He didn't even say I'd hit him. I guess he'd just wanted to look the big man in front of his friends. My lawyer had a defence of provocation ready, but the judge said there was no case to answer. He had the case thrown out of court and made an oblique comment about the police force bringing far too many petty charges to court.'

'That must have been a huge relief.'

'I can't tell you how much. The judge said the police sergeant in charge of the two policemen should apologise to me in person. It was that bloke there was all the fuss about, the first black sergeant. But I've not seen hide nor hair of him. Kelly rang the station, to ask what was happening, and they said he'd been transferred. The only good thing was that the kids stopped coming round the neighbourhood.'

'It must have been about the time we opened this club,' said Joe. 'Maybe some of them started to come here.'

'And that's the thing,' said Nick. 'I found another job, but I also got to thinking. What could I do to help the kids, to give them something to do with their time instead of frightening old ladies. I saw your advert, so here I am'.

. . .

In the police canteen, Brian bit into a second chocolate digestive.

'The one course I did understand, he said, 'was the one that got me into deep water. It sounded weird when you first heard it, but it made sense if you thought about it. If you want a good conviction record, don't go for the criminal bastards because they can worm their way out of anything. Go for the law-abiding types instead. You know where they live and they're not going to bugger off. And they don't know how to lie so you've got them banged to rights.'

Bill looked uncomfortable. He had been in the force for a long time. He believed the police should serve the public. He was unhappy with the target culture and he listened to Brian with a growing sense of unease.

Brian took no notice. 'My squad didn't respect me,' he continued, 'but they did like me. I'm a likeable fellow, what can I say? So when I came up with this idea for improving performance with less effort, they jumped at the chance. We doubled our arrest rate in the first week, mostly vehicle-related but who cares? I didn't need to tell them to go easy on the kids. These days, kids can get away with murder, so why bother wasting your time?'

Bill frowned. 'So how did you end up here?' he asked.

'It all went wrong. Prosecuting a bloke for assault when he's taking a stick off a kid seems easy, but you want to be sure there isn't a video to support the defence. And the kid must have some sort of mark on him.'

'So that's what happened,' said Bill.

'The chief constable transferred me here. My job's to collect data and pass it on to the CRB for their checks. He's been waiting to see if that bloke will bring a case against us, but he's not the type. He'll just want to get on with his life and not make a fuss. A bit like me, I suppose, when I was on

56

the beat. Anyway, the chief constable rang me earlier. He says we're in the clear. He says I mustn't cock up the CRB job.'

. . .

Five months after his meeting in the community centre, Nick picked up the telephone.

'I've bad news,' said Joe. 'Your CRB check has come through. An assault on a minor precludes you from working with kids – even if you're not convicted. I'm really sorry.'

Nick went into the kitchen. Kelly put her arms round him.

'Where's the sense in that?' she said.

The Priest and the Altar Boy

In which the LUSTFUL priest goes unpunished
while the altar boy's love turns to dust

Blue lights were flashing on two police cars and an ambulance. They were drawn up outside a large Victorian house on the outskirts of Reading which had been converted into bedsits several decades earlier. Paint was peeling off the window frames; patches of render had fallen off the front façade.

The house was home to a number of manual and clerical workers, single men who failed to qualify for social housing. They had drifted into this backwater because they found it hard to make friends or fit into the world. They had little to do with each other, passing each other on the stairs with a muttered 'good morning' or 'goodnight'.

It was the smell from the largest room on the first floor that forced them to talk to each other. The room was occupied by a new tenant whom none of them had seen, let alone spoken to. They finally plucked up courage to knock on the door, quietly at first, then increasingly loudly. There was no answer. Muttering that it would be wrong to force the door open, the tenants drifted away into their own rooms.

The smell worsened during the next few days until one of the tenants telephoned the landlord. It was he who found Michael's decomposing body inside the room. The landlord had little information to add. Michael had answered his advertisement in the newsagent's window. He had paid a deposit and three months' rent in advance, so there had been no need for a reference.

As the paramedics transferred the remains into a body bag, a policeman rifled through Michael's wallet and found the address of his parents. Arriving in Reading the following morning, his father identified the body, while his mother sat

59

in the waiting room, her head in her hands.

. . .

As a child, Michael was his mother's pride and joy. His father
– a plumber from Ireland, his rigid view of life stiffened by
stout and whisky – made sure he was a good boy. His wife
kept a low profile on Friday and Saturday nights, keeping out
of his way when he came home drunk from the pub. She
came into her own on Sundays, taking Michael with her as
she walked to and from the church of Our Lady of Miracles.
On Saints Days, all three of them went to church, a rare
demonstration of family solidarity. And her heart filled with
pride when Michael became an altar boy.

He was an intelligent and well-behaved child but he was
not popular at school. His mother assured him that this was
because he was clever and that other boys were jealous. It did
not matter, she said, that he was no good at sport. But to
Michael it did matter. He felt scorned. And the constant
derision made him feel lonely and withdrawn.

His life began to change when he was twelve. Lying in the
bath one evening, he felt a strange sensation. He looked down
and saw that his penis was longer and thicker than usual. He
stretched his hand out and touched it tentatively. The
sensation was not unpleasant – rather the opposite. Confused
by this new strangeness, he was relieved when his mother
called to tell him his tea was ready.

In the weeks that followed, he became accustomed to
waking up most mornings with an erection. He told no-one
and, as spring turned into summer, the school made its first
visit to the local swimming pool. He was expecting humiliation
as he proved inadequate in another field of physical
endeavour – but the embarrassment that overwhelmed him in
the changing room was beyond anything he could have
imagined.

It was a big open space with no partitions to block the
field of view as in the school locker rooms. Like him, most of
the other boys were around puberty and, as Michael's eyes
moved over their tight buttocks, their sculpted back muscles,
their firm thighs, his penis grew and swelled. Overcome with
a powerful emotion, he covered himself up as best he could

before the cold water in the pool doused his embarrassment. But from that moment he knew for sure: he was attracted by men and not by women. He also knew, altar boy that he was, that this was against the will of God.

As he applied himself to his school work, he tried not to think about sex. But he was often in contact with the other boys and he found it difficult to control his feelings. In the sweet shop, his eyes were drawn to the top shelf of the magazine section, to the cover pictures of half-naked men with alluring smiles. He did not have the courage to take one in his hands and open the pages. And he was too young to buy a copy.

Walking alone through the streets one Saturday afternoon, he saw a magazine lying among the bushes. It was a little muddy but the image of a strong male body on the front cover attracted his attention. He inserted it under his sweater, carried it home and locked himself in the toilet to read it.

His mother would notice if he stayed there too long, so he rationed himself. At first, he concentrated on the pictures: the firm muscle tone, the tight buttocks, the smooth thighs and the semi-erect penises, exceptionally long and thick. He taught himself to masturbate and was careful to have toilet paper available to leave no trace. He lacked the courage to look at the magazine in bed – but the recollection of the images brought him excitement and pleasure which surpassed anything he had felt before.

When he had looked at the pictures, he began to read the articles. There was an erotic story with details of oral sex and sodomy. There were articles about gay liberation and how the age of consent should be lowered. And as he read, his predicament worsened. He knew what he was doing was a sin in God's eyes, but he could not understand how something that gave so much pleasure and which came so naturally could be considered so wrong.

He was good at covering his traces, of avoiding topics of conversation that threatened to reveal his feelings. He lived in the confines of the closet he had made for himself. At the same time, masturbation was a constant pleasure. He was frustrated by the lack of new magazines, but he had a lively imagination and could generate his own fantasies. He applied himself to his school work and did well in examinations, but he learned to keep a low profile when playing sport to attract less attention from the other boys.

His weekly confession with Father Dermot was a problem. He had been brought up to be a good Catholic and the requirement to confess and atone for his sins had been drummed into him since early childhood. He could not give up his new-found pleasures – which he would be required to do if he confessed them to Father Dermot. So he kept them to himself, confessing only minor sins at school.

. . .

His life changed again soon after his sixteenth birthday. After his regular visit to the sweet shop, where he browsed the top shelf of the magazine rack before buying a copy of *History Today* for himself and *Woman's Own* for his mother, a man in his early thirties approached him in the street and made a comment about the weather. He said his name was Simon and he had seen Michael in the shop. He asked how long Michael had been interested in history and why he had bought a copy of *Woman's Own*. Michael answered in monosyllables, but the man was friendly and soon he began to feel more comfortable. When they reached the bakery, the man suggested a coffee and a doughnut in the cafe at the back of the shop.

Years of living in the shadows had honed Simon's sensitivity to the character of others. He could see that Michael was gay, intelligent and inexperienced. He opened the conversation by asking the real reason for Michael's visits to the sweet shop. Then he made coded allusions to Michael's sexual interests. He had grown up at a time when the tastes that he and Michael shared could only be sampled furtively and secretly – except for the moneyed or the artistic elite who seemed to get away with most things – and was accustomed to being discreet. But Michael had no trouble detecting the secret messages that his words carried in this public place.

Invited to visit Simon a few days later, Michael became increasingly excited as the time approached. And as he walked through Simon's front door, a whole new world opened up. Simon was interested in everything about him. He sympathised with his lack of ability at sport. He talked about Michael's favourite subjects at school and was knowledgeable about history, music, literature and art. He introduced him to his library of books. It was an easy step from opening a book of Michelangelo sculptures to opening the door to Simon's bedroom.

Michael was happy to lose his virginity to a gentle sensitive man whose sensuality matched his own. A real passion entered his life. At the same time, he found a mentor whose love and care helped him to develop his understanding of the world of music, art and literature. He felt himself blossom – and he delayed what he knew would be his last confession. He had to keep silent about his new life, while telling Father Dermot that he no longer wished to be an altar boy. The forthcoming examinations, he explained, would leave him with no time for church duties.

Father Dermot accepted the explanation, expressing the hope that Michael would continue to attend Mass every Sunday. Two hours later, he listened to another confession, this time from a young woman who – like Michael – had just reached the age of sixteen.

. . .

Father Dermot had been brought up by his mother. His father, a merchant seaman, had abandoned her as soon as she told him of her pregnancy. This had given her a jaundiced view of men – which she made no effort to conceal.

Her group of friends were women who discussed and derided their partners and condemned men in general, often in Dermot's hearing. He grew up with the idea that men were the inferior sex, that men had nothing to contribute to the world. When he discovered a sexual interest in girls, he perceived it as shameful. He did not believe that any girl could be interested in him. But he still had lustful feelings and he spent his days trying to hide his interest in the female bodies all around him. All women were in focus for him and all were desirable. Men were part of the background scenery, like the grass and the trees.

He did try to talk to girls, but he was maladroit and they found him creepy. He could see the contempt on their faces. Frustrated, miserable and confused, he found salvation in the church. He could see that priests, with their black clothes and dog-collars, were not like other men. Their role gave them respect, while priestly celibacy offered a lifeline to a young man unsure of his masculinity and afraid of women.

He enrolled in the seminary where he learned to keep his sexual feelings under control. He felt less alone and was particularly cheered by the deference shown to him by young nuns who were working as domestic servants. Dermot was attracted by their youth and felt virtuous when he resisted the temptation to touch them. Best of all, he was training to be a superior being, a policemen of the souls of others. This role was determined, not by his own nature, but by the power vested in him by the church.

Dermot passed through the seminary, was ordained priest, and started work in the parish of Our Lady of Miracles. And two hours after agreeing that Michael could give up his duties as an altar boy, he listened to Mary's confession.

. . .

Mary too had had a sexual awakening. She too had discovered masturbation. She was overwhelmed and frightened by the sensations and emotions it unleashed, and felt a need for spiritual guidance. So when knelt in the confessional to confess her sins, it seemed to Father Dermot that his moment had come. He no longer had to be maladroit, he did not have to stammer or stumble over ill-chosen words. He asked if she would like to have tea in the vestry. And it was in the vestry that he placed an avuncular hand on her knee.

Mary was surprised. But at the same time, she was flattered that this man of authority should be so interested in her. A priest, she knew, would not stray from the righteous path. There was a fumbling, an adjustment of clothing, then it was over. Father Dermot warned her not to talk of what had happened, to tell no-one. He knew she would obey.

A few weeks later, Mary's family moved away from the area. She left the parish without regrets. She felt that she had become a woman.

During the next year, Father Dermot had two further encounters with parishioners in his care, one in the vestry and one at the altar. The girls were sixteen and seventeen years old. They were untidy episodes and both girls were overcome with guilt. The second encounter ended when he felt the need to threaten dire consequences if the girl told her parents. No-one would believe her, he said. Then he began an affair with a novice in the convent where he acted as spiritual supervisor. This satisfied his needs for several months until the novice moved to a convent in a different parish.

. . .

Meanwhile, the relationship between Michael and Simon had blossomed. With Simon as his tutor, Michael did well in all his examinations. His head teacher suggested that he should apply for Oxford or Cambridge.

Michael visited Simon whenever he could, unaware that Simon's neighbour was watching him coming and going. The neighbour could see that Michael was still at school, below the age of gay sexual consent. He began spying on the house when Michael was visiting and noticed that the bedroom curtains were drawn for some time during each visit. So he telephoned the police.

The report landed on the desk of a police sergeant, an evangelical Christian who shared the neighbour's belief that homosexuality was a sin. She drove herself to Simon's house. The bedroom curtains were closed. Ten minutes later, Michael and Simon were in the back of the police car.

Soon everyone knew: Michael's parents, his teachers, the other boys at school. It was Wednesday so, although his father was furious, he kept his hands by his sides. He agreed with his wife that they should seek Father Dermot's advice. And Father Dermot, following the Vatican line, recommended a Catholic mental hospital which used aversion therapy as a treatment for homosexuality.

Simon was given a six months' suspended sentence on condition that he should not attempt to see Michael. And Michael, his new-found confidence in ruins, agreed to the aversion therapy. This proved to be nasty, painful and humiliating, but his father insisted he continue if he wanted to remain at home with his family.

During the next year, Michael lost interest in his studies. He left school and moved to Reading, where he found a clerical job and rented a room on the first floor of a run-down Victorian house on the edge of the town.

. . .

Nuala was a neurotic girl given to hysterical outbursts. Father Dermot should have stopped as soon as she started to shake when he put his hand on her knee. He should have taken the hint when she struggled and snivelled as he touched her breasts. But he was feeling confident because his earlier encounters had been so easy. He tried to calm her afterwards, but neither threats nor soothing words could stop her wailing. He knew he would soon be in trouble.

Nuala's parents were hard-line Catholics of the old school. They blamed Nuala as much as they blamed Father Dermot. They reported the matter to the bishop, who consulted his superiors in Rome and was persuaded to hush up the story.

Father Dermot, bribed by the promise that the police would not be informed, confessed to his other encounters. The bishop wrote down the girls' names, so the diocese would be forewarned if there were other complaints, but he did nothing to contact their parents. He offered Nuala's parents a free place in a convent school which had high academic standards and a reputation for discipline. He warned the school that Nuala tended to fantasise and had been known to make false accusations. And Father Dermot was quietly moved to a parish in Western Australia. No record of his misdeeds followed him there.

. . .

A few weeks after his arrival in Australia, Father Dermot received a letter from Michael's parents, forwarded from the church of Our Lady of Miracles.

The letter told him about Michael's suicide in the Victorian house in Reading. It explained that there would be no funeral because he had chosen to take his own life. It thanked Father Dermot for all he had done to rescue their son from the path of evil.

And Simon, who had read of Michael's death in the local newspaper, spent the rest of his life nursing a broken heart.

The Woman who would be King

PRIDE, they say, goes before a fall; but we're still waiting

As Dorothy sat behind a large mahogany desk waiting for her next meeting, she gave thought to the legacy she hoped to leave behind. She was not the first female prime minister of the country, so she would need to work hard to make her mark. And she knew that some decisions, easy to make, could sometimes lead to an outpouring of public approbation. The next meeting – the kind she loved most – would provide her with just such an opportunity. She had already decided on the outcome.

After a knock at the door, a small delegation was ushered into the room: the gaunt parents, their solicitor, and the director of the hastily-formed Association for the Elimination of Dangerous Dogs. The newspapers were full of the story of the small girl savaged by two terriers in a public park. The mother had also been bitten as she tried to rescue her daughter. A police marksman stunned the dogs with tranquilizer darts before they were loaded into a van and removed from the scene. The ambulance took longer to arrive; the child died on the way to hospital.

After the obligatory exchange of condolences, Dorothy said all the right things. 'I shall use everything in my power,' she said, 'to make sure that nothing like this will ever happen again.'

When the meeting was over, her media adviser opened the door between their two offices.

'Hello Jack,' she said. 'That went well. I haven't changed my mind. We'll introduce the bill to threaten owners who fail to control their dogs. I suggest a minimum of five years in prison. Parents shouldn't be afraid to let their children play in public parks.'

This would be the third piece of legislation that Dorothy

enacted in response to public outrage. She enjoyed doing this. She had grown up hearing her father in his strong Scouser's voice: 'They should lock 'em up and throw away the key'. The words were etched in her memory, her father's ideas of justice never far from her thoughts. She threw the briefing note she had been given into her out-tray on top of a copy of the *Daily Mail*. The briefing note had pointed out that similar incidents were rare and that defining 'control of dogs' would be difficult. But depending on the definition used, between 5 and 375 people a year were likely to fall foul of the proposed law.

Dorothy had a clear sense of what she could achieve in terms of pleasing the public. She was a better politician than her colleagues because she realised that a weak moral compass was essential to effective leadership. She could appear bright and enthusiastic about everything she backed, whether she believed in it or not. She could change her mind in public without turning a hair. Above all, she could play to the crowd. She was comfortable in the world of the half-truth, the quarter-truth, and the lie.

But none of this would ensure her legacy. For this she needed Jack, who was better at strategic, long-term thinking. She could latch onto ideas, such as a hospital building programme. What better legacy than a health service endowed with monuments in steel, glass and concrete? She also leapt at the idea of a school building programme, which minimised the drain on resources by using private companies to carry the burden of costs. The state would lease the schools from the builders, so the bulk of the payments would be made by her successors. These schemes provided the public with visible demonstrations of her good intentions. At the same time, she could continue to restrict her already-stretched budget for the supply and salaries of nurses and teachers.

Dorothy tended to lose interest after she had floated an idea. It was left to her second-rate ministers to follow them through. They were good at spending money but they rarely thought about the consequences. Their actions were driven by short-term expediency. And Dorothy was always coming up with new ideas, each new thought driving the last one from her mind.

. . .

My darling Ernie,

We heard today about the helicopter crash which killed the crew. Was that from your squadron? You know we worry about you all the time.

Your Susie is not in a good shape. I know you looked after each other since you were nippers, especially since your Mum died. I've never known a brother and sister so close. But now you're over there, she wants to keep you from worrying. So don't tell her I told you.

That boyfriend of hers was locked up after his dog ran off and frightened a bunch of kids coming out of school. So now Susie's got no money. She's been to the Social but it'll be weeks till the cash comes through. How's she going to cope till then? A man came from the council to ask her questions. It was his job, he said, to make sure the council didn't pay her a penny more than it had to. Your Granddad is giving her some of our winter fuel money.

I took Granddad to the hospital on Friday. He's being put on something called warfarin and there are loads of tests. The ambulance picked us up at half past seven. The new hospital looks lovely, clean and bright. After he had the tests, we had to hang about all morning before they prescribed the right dose. Then we hung around most of the afternoon waiting for an ambulance to take us home. We had no lunch because we didn't dare leave the waiting room in case we missed it. We'd already missed one because we weren't been told where to go. It was half past six before we were taken home. They were going to leave me behind the ambulance was full and I wasn't a patient. The driver took pity on me when I started to cry. He let me on but told me to keep quiet about it. By then, I was fed up with the new hospital.

Look after yourself and take care. We think about you all the time.

Love, Gran.

. . .

Jack had spent his whole career in the media. He had many enemies in the press and was not a forgiving man. He was

71

pulled in two directions; he was tempted to settle old scores but, at the same time, his job was to ensure that journalists were happy. He usually achieved the right balance – but not always.

When the peace talks which led to reduced violence in Northern Ireland were successful, he pushed Dorothy into the limelight and side-lined the minister who had done all the hard work. But his attention was diverted at the critical moment when rumours emerged of sex scandal involving another minister. Jack gave all his attention to burying the rumours, leaving the story of Dorothy the peacemaker without sufficient coverage.

Dorothy was partly to blame. She could have given Jack firm instructions, but her mind was elsewhere at the time. She revelled in the reflected glory of being seen with the powerful and the glitterati. It was not just their company she craved: she enjoyed their gifts and their flattering kindnesses, the luxury holidays in Europe and in jet-set resorts around the world. She would sit in meetings and think about visits to palaces and villas and cruises on expensive yachts. She was proud of herself for having come so far and having achieved so much – but it drew her attention away from the matter in hand and Jack, her most trusted adviser, was left to his own devices.

Sometimes, as she attended meetings when important decisions were made, she would realise that her mind had wandered, that she had heard little of the debate. And instead of weighing evidence which had been painstakingly gathered and carefully presented, her instinct was to shoot from the hip. She was confident that her personality, her cunning, and above all her willingness to lie, would carry her through. She could always rely on Jack to extricate her from any problems that arose.

This was how she agreed to the idea that an increased number of prisoners should be released on parole. The meeting was long and tedious. She had hoped to avoid it but the home secretary insisted. It began with a discussion of overcrowding and the fact that many new prisoners had to start their sentences in police cells. When the discussion turned to prisoners' rights and the danger of mixing different categories of prisoner, her mind wandered to a villa in the Caribbean. She missed the presentation on the cost of providing new prison accommodation and only took notice when an official mentioned that money could be saved by early release. This grabbed her attention. Voters are uninterested in the building of prisons, she thought. But they like the idea of saving money.

'So that's what we'll do,' she said. 'We'll put together a plan for early release.'

. . .

Dear Ernie,

We've had such a to-do in the street. Mrs Brandon from no 21 has been killed – a burglary which went wrong. If her husband hadn't got up to go to the toilet it wouldn't have happened. You know he's had problems with his waterworks. He's been waiting to go into hospital for eleven months. He disturbed the burglar who'd come in through the toilet window. He knocked Mr Brandon down and, when Mrs Brandon got up to see what was happening, he took a swipe at her. She fell and hit her head on the skirting.

There's a rumour that the burglar was let out of prison early because of overcrowding. They put people like Susie's boyfriend in prison for not keeping dogs on a lead. Then they get overcrowding and let out the real villains instead.

I know Susie's written to tell you what happened to her little boy – but I don't think she told you the details. It's a real shame. Her money hadn't come through, so she got a cleaning job. She shouldn't have left the boy by himself, but it was early in the morning and he was usually asleep. The Social have taken him away for neglect. Nothing Susie could say would change their minds. What's she to do if she's got no money? I don't like her bloke but at least he was bringing cash into the house.

Your Granddad is still going to the hospital a couple of times a week. I don't go with him now in case they won't bring me home.

Look after yourself, Love, Gran

. . .

When news broke about the early-release prisoner who had broken into a house, assaulted the householder and killed his wife – 'Home Office let criminals back on the street' – Jack strained every sinew to down-play Dorothy's involvement. He had compiled dossiers on everyone with power in the country, men and women. He was inspired by J. Edgar Hoover of the FBI, whose methods (lots of stick and not much carrot) became his guiding light when Dorothy employed him as her media adviser. Aware that the home secretary had a roving eye, it was easy to discover the name of his latest attachment. He then tipped off a friend who worked at one of the sleazier newspapers.

The scandal hit the press the morning after the story about the killing. It was a simple matter to persuade the home secretary to take the blame for the early release policy, as well as a whole raft of other home office problems. Dorothy was in the clear and, a short time later, a terrorist attack in the United States drove domestic politics off the front pages.

While leaders of other countries kept their distance as much as they dared, perceiving the US president to be ignorant and self-serving, Dorothy snatched the moment, becoming the first world leader to make a public statement of sympathy and support. She was also the first to commit troops to support his cause and was soon drawn into his plan to extend war across the Middle East.

She did not like the president, but she was aware of his power and huge personal wealth. She had flattered him since his election to the Oval Office, and now she saw an opportunity to ensure her legacy. Prime ministers in wartime tend to be popular – and how could she fail as the closest friend of the most powerful man in the world?

Her greatest contribution to the president's war effort was to ensure that Jack provided an excuse to extend his involvement deeper into the Middle East by massaging the intelligence data. As a result, she received an unprecedented welcome when she travelled to the States and addressed the American Congress. It was arranged that her son would be given a place at a top American university; other benefits were discussed but would be held over until she left government.

Dorothy's international profile grew as she embarked on a tour of capital cities around the world, trying to persuade other governments to join the president's the cause. Few were willing to refuse outright – even fewer were as enthusiastic as Dorothy. But she was adept at closing her ears to criticism, particularly when veiled in diplomatic language. She convinced herself that her world trip had been a success.

At home, her ministers were docile, despite a huge public demonstration against the war. Jack ensured that the reasons for the home secretary's resignation were well understood by politicians. The decision to go to war was passed by parliament with only token reservations.

. . .

Dear Ernie,

Your Granddad and I are worried about you. We know you signed up to be a soldier but fighting in the desert is hard. Your Granddad was a Desert Rat and he says that sand gets everywhere. When he and his mates were out there, they knew what they were fighting for. They looked up to Churchill. And back home, we all worked together. It's not like that now. The government has been accused of lying, people have lost their jobs, and some expert or other has killed himself. And your Granddad says you should never have been given boots that hurt your feet. It's in all the newspapers that the equipment isn't good enough.

Susie got her boy back on Friday. It's taken five months to get him out of the care home. It happened when they went to court and the judge told the Social to stop being stupid. He asked them what Susie was supposed to do if she had no money. He said it would be a good thing if more people tried to look after themselves. Susie's worried now that the Social will take her flat away from her out of spite.

Write back and tell us you're all right so we don't have to worry. We will worry – but write anyway.

Love, Gran.

. . .

The war in the Middle East went well and was soon labelled as a great victory. The enemy – which Jack's 'intelligence' had described as a massive threat to the West – had no strength to defend itself. Although the war was unpopular at home, particularly when body bags began arriving at the airbase, Dorothy was enjoying herself. She flew around the globe and was praised by world leaders for her leadership and courage.

Although the enemy had been easily defeated, it proved more difficult to restore order on the ground. Dissident factions had arisen, foreign groups were making incursions into the country, and violence began to spread. Money was needed to equip the army but Dorothy disliked spending money unless it enhanced her reputation. As a result, she approved every scheme available which could help to reduce costs.

At one cabinet meeting, there were two items on the agenda: whether to order better armoured vehicles for use in the Middle East or to abandon a major IT project in the health service. There were problems with the IT project, which the contractor blamed on the civil service changing the specifications almost every month. The total cost of cancelling the project was roughly similar to the cost of the improved armoured vehicles.

Dorothy found the decision easy to make.

. . .

Dear Ernie,

We're so happy you've landed a cushy number. When we read your letter about how you go every week with your officer to collect a suitcase full of money from the Americans and spend the rest of the week taking it to the ministers that run the electricity and the hospitals. Granddad said it was a funny way to run a war. But you still need to look after yourself. There was something on television last night about how your armoured cars aren't strong enough and how the government won't give you better ones. Granddad says it wasn't like that in his day.

Take care. We want you home in one piece.

Love, Gran.

. . .

Two weeks later, Ernie's grandparents opened the letter they had been expecting since the late-night telephone call a few days earlier. It was neatly typed and expressed regret that their grandson had been killed when his armoured vehicle had been destroyed by a roadside bomb. Dorothy had signed the letter with a flourish, taking pride in the strength and character of her signature.

On the same day, the newspaper headlines were dominated by the revelation that British soldiers had mistreated Middle-Eastern prisoners in detention camps and that CIA aircraft had used British airports as staging posts in the transport of suspects to interrogation facilities in North Africa.

Buried on an inside page, they also reported that the prime minister had recently purchased an Elizabethan mansion in Suffolk.

From the Geyser Ventilators

In the hands of the ENVIOUS,

even petty power becomes a weapon

Lying in her warm bath, Kathy looked up through the roof-light, watching the clouds drift across the sky. Today was her 68th birthday. The postman had not yet arrived – but she was not expecting any cards.

Her morning bath was the most comfortable time of her day. The gas fire in her little sitting room failed to give out enough warmth. Facing north, the room never filled with sunlight and the window looked out on a dreary street of Victorian houses on the edge of London. Her bedroom window faced a brick wall. In her bath at least, Kathy could sometimes see blue sky.

Her life had been comfortable until she moved into this small flat. She had married an accountant and they lived in a pleasant suburban house with a large garden. Few middle-class women went out to work at that time and Kathy was content to be a housewife. She worked hard in the house and created a beautiful garden.

Her husband was a conventional man, but he liked to travel and they enjoyed more exotic holidays than was usual for the 1970s, to America, North Africa and the Far East. These helped to compensate for the lack of children in their marriage and, rather late in the day, they tried to adopt. They filled in the forms and waited for an interview. Then they were told that they were too old – Kathy at 35, Ed at 40 – to be adoptive parents. More importantly, Ed was a smoker and it had been decided to ban smokers from adopting children. Surely, said Ed, children would be better off in a loving home with a bit of cigarette smoke than being placed in a care home. Besides, most care-home workers smoked and kids were bound to try cigarettes behind the bike sheds. But there was no argument, no appeal.

So Kathy began working for a charity which supported

children in difficult circumstances: poverty, abusive families, fathers in prison, mothers addicted to drugs or alcohol. She became a surrogate mother to some of the children and a caring friend to the families of others. She did her work conscientiously and well, but she was not one to blow her own trumpet and her efforts went largely unnoticed by anyone except those she helped. She won no awards. But she found the work fulfilling and was happy to know that she had helped a little.

When Ed retired, he and Kathy decided to spend more time travelling. Their large garden required constant attention, so they put the house on the market and moved to a smaller property, a 17th-century cottage in a nearby village with stone walls, stone tiled roof, exposed beams and an inglenook fireplace. It was a listed building and they loved its eccentricities. It even had roses around the front door. There was enough space in the small garden for chairs and a table, and Kathy brought colour into the garden with flowerbeds and pots.

She was widowed within a year of Ed's retirement and two days after returning from a trip in a camper-van across the United States and through the Canadian Rockies. Ed was driving to the supermarket to buy a carton of milk. He was waiting to turn into the main road when a police car driven at 90 mph hit his car from behind and pushed it into the path of a lorry. Ed was killed, as well as the police driver who had just passed his professional driving test and was trying out his new skills. An enquiry was held but, since two of the witnesses were dead and the lorry driver, affected by severe concussion, had no recollection of the incident, it reached no conclusion. It merely advised the police to exercise more caution when driving at high speed.

A few months after Ed's funeral, the roof of the cottage began to leak. Kathy called in a surveyor who reported that the roof was in poor condition and needed extensive repair. He recommended that the stone tiles be removed, new roofing felt installed, and the tiles re-hung. It would be an expensive job.

Kathy was concerned about the cost, particularly since

there was a problem with Ed's pension. The respected and long-standing insurance company entrusted with his savings had been involved in a protracted court case and the verdict had not been in its favour. Successive appeals failed, after which it was discovered that the company had overstated its assets and under-reported its liabilities. It was therefore unable to pay out the pensions it had promised. Efforts to shame the government into making up the shortfall failed, even when an independent report pointed out serious failures in the regulator's oversight.

So Kathy would be poorer than she had expected. She had not been involved with their finances while Ed was alive, but she worked out that she could, with some difficulty, scrape together the money to pay for the roof repairs. And if she was frugal, she could continue to live in her cottage with the colourful garden that she loved so much.

. . .

In a similar flat two streets away, Heather also soaked in her bath and looked up at the clouds through the roof-light. Soon she would have to climb out of the bath and set off for work.

She had been a spoilt child, her father calling her his little princess. She had grown up expecting things to be done for her, an attitude which she copied from her mother. She was a pretty child and bright enough to do well at school and then at college. She found employment in an office where she took excellent care of her nail varnish. Then she found a husband to look after her.

Heather was attractive to men. Her mother had taught her to play hard to get and she learnt to use sex as a means of getting her own way. Nicholas was inadequate, his self-confidence shattered by his mother. Heather's strong personality made him feel comfortable. It was a relationship he understood. The humiliation of being denied sex made him strive to mollify her and Heather found it easy to control the relationship.

Nicholas ran a small wholesale firm that provided him with a comfortable living but, after several years of marriage, a run of bad debts forced the business into bankruptcy. He had to sell the house to repay the bank loan. Heather could not bear the shame and, since Nicholas could no longer provide her with the life she wanted, she divorced him. There was almost no money to be shared between them. She could only just afford to buy herself the little flat with the roof-light above the bath.

Heather felt bewildered. This was not what she had expected of the world. And playing hard-to-get was proving less successful now she was older. Disappointment drew dark lines beneath her eyes and at the corners of her mouth. Few men asked her out – and those who did found her needy. A string of short-lived relationships eroded her confidence. It seemed so unfair that those around her lived better lives. She found herself a group of female friends in similar circumstances. They would talk about how badly they were treated.

The one good thing in her life was a new job. In an effort to meet people, she had joined an evening class on the architecture of older buildings. Then she had seen an advertisement for a conservation officer in the local council. She had neither experience of the work nor a suitable qualification, but there were no other applicants and a reference from her evening class tutor was considered sufficient.

Heather enjoyed the job because it gave her power. There were few rules to guide her decisions. It was easy to find reasons to refuse applications or impose restrictions which made it difficult to implement the work or made a project less satisfactory. Her decisions were inconsistent. She turned down an application to erect a well-designed and elegant porch on the grounds that 'it was not in keeping with the style of the building'. She also turned down an application for the demolition of an unsightly porch on the grounds that 'the modernisation projects of the 1960s should be retained for historical purposes'. The people whose dreams she held in her hands had better lives than her own. And every time she turned down an application, she felt that she was getting a little of her own back.

Heather's decisions were little different from those of her colleagues. Architects accustomed to listed-building applications knew it was wise to include at least one outrageous element; in this way, the Aunt Sally would raise questions while the rest of the project would go through on the nod. So although Heather's behaviour was unexceptional, she did get an extra thrill, a buzzing in her loins which made up for the sexual pleasure she had denied herself.

At her interview, she had agreed to go on as many courses as possible to make up for her lack of qualifications. Even so, her lack of knowledge caused problems. She would insist on builders using techniques she had read about but did not fully understand, techniques impracticable for the job in hand. As a result, architects and builders learnt to treat her gently, easing her into amending her decisions without calling attention to her ignorance.

One of the courses she attended was about roof construction through the ages. She learnt about the use of ship's timbers and roof beams joined together by wooden pegs, and was particularly taken by the hand-made nails that were used before modern nails became available. The lecturer brought some old nails for his students to hold in their hands. Heather thought they looked beautiful.

. . .

Kathy's application to carry out repairs to her roof of her listed cottage landed on Heather's desk a few days after she attended the course on roof construction. Heather visited the cottage to inspect the roof and was offered tea in the garden. Kathy did not tell Heather about Ed's death or the problems with his pension scheme. Instead, she talked about her flowers and how much she loved her garden. Then they went inside where she pointed out the damp patches on the ceilings and explained the proposed work to the roof.

Heather thought how happy she would be if she lived in Kathy's cottage. And she felt a flush of pleasure when she noticed the nails that had been used in the original construction. A few weeks later, she drafted the planning permission for the work to Kathy's roof, adding a condition that hand-made nails be used 'to preserve the character of the building'.

When Kathy first read the letter from the council, she

failed to appreciate its implications. But when her surveyor explained that the use of hand-made nails would almost double the cost of the work, she broke down in tears. She did not have the stamina to fight. Her budget was already stretched; she could not afford the extra cost.

The cottage was put up for sale. With a defective roof and the punitive condition in the planning permission, she had no choice but to reduce the price significantly. As a result, she could only afford the little flat with the skylight. She had lost her garden, but she could still take pleasure from the clouds above her as she lay in her bath.

Two streets away, Heather thought no more about Kathy's cottage. She had moved on. There were more applications to reject, more punitive conditions to impose. Every morning, she too lay in her bath and watched the clouds – but they brought her no joy.

. . .

The title of this story is taken from the first line of 'Business Girls' by John Betjeman. Reading the poem, I thought about the women lying in their baths and looking up at the clouds and wondered what they might be thinking about.